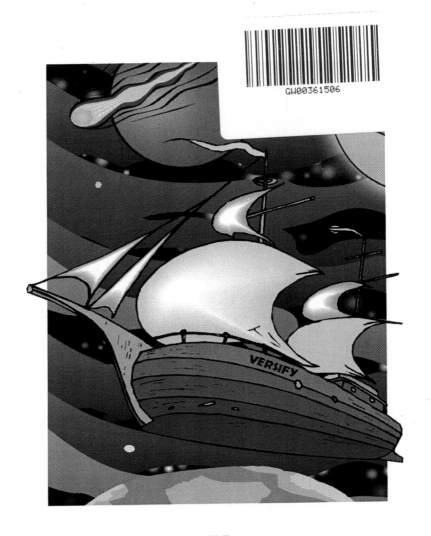

POETIC VOYAGES
NORTH HAMPSHIRE

Edited by Allison Dowse

First published in Great Britain in 2001 by
YOUNG WRITERS
Remus House,
Coltsfoot Drive,
Peterborough, PE2 9JX
Telephone (01733) 890066

HB ISBN 0 75433 278 0
SB ISBN 0 75433 279 9

FOREWORD

Young Writers was established in 1991 with the aim
to promote creative writing in children, to make
reading and writing poetry fun.

This year once again, proved to be a tremendous
success with over 88,000 entries received nationwide.

The Poetic Voyages competition has shown us the
high standard of work and effort that children are
capable of today. It is a reflection of the teaching
skills in schools, the enthusiasm and creativity they
have injected into their pupils shines clearly within
this anthology.

The task of selecting poems was therefore a difficult
one but nevertheless, an enjoyable experience. We
hope you are as pleased with the final selection in
Poetic Voyages North Hampshire as we are.

CONTENTS

James Wilkins	71
Catherine Raggett	71
Catherine O'Farrell	72
Emilie Bergström	72
Sophie Farelly	73
Thomas Smart	73
Rebecca Harman	74

St Peter's CE Junior School, Farnborough

Rebecca McNutt	74
Rebecca Attridge	75
Sarah Dunford	76
Abigail Burch	77
Alexandra Tulip	78
George Barker	78
Christopher Wenham	79
Emma Browne	79
Charlotte Byrne	80
Alan Phelan	80
Rebekah Williams	81
Rebecca Cagney	82
Kate Stallard	82
Charlotte Johnson	83
James Cagney	83
Peter Marron	84
Samuel Jones	84
Bryna Godar	85
Donna Quincey	85
Oliver Johnston	86

South Farnborough Junior School

Rikki Brittin	86
Sam Pool	87
Rhiannon Harrison	88
William Sterry	89
Jessica Castle	90
Chantal Comeau	90
Avril Judge	91

Emma Haynes	92
Samantha Warner	93
Becky Stamp	94
Mercedes Bennett	94
Sophie Cush	95
Yolanda Wynn	95
Jack Price	96
Jack Davis Brewer	96
Louise Harding	97
Declan Pollock	98
Chloé Darrah-Cliffe	98
Adrian Earle	99
Robert Harral	100
Kurtis Wayne-Scaife	100
Steven Schafer	101
Tiffany Walker	101
Craig Andrew Scoular	102
Lucy North	102
Morgan King	103
David Jones	103
Robert Murray	104
Robert Harding	104
Hannah Bryant	105
Emily Hazeldine	106
Aimée Davison	106
Shaun Tobin	107
Sophia Jarvis	108
Jessica Berry	108
David Pitkin	109
Steven Izzard	109
Poppie Turner	110
Josie Wyatt	110
Stacie Humm	111
Phoebe Coffey	111
Hazel Oakes	112
Samantha Mason	113

The Poems

A WORM'S DREAM

A worm dreams of growing wings,
And flying with Prince Charles,
Past Westlife performing their number one hit,
And a bawling little child.

He dreams of flying over clouds,
And under London Bridge,
Past the Queen knighting 'Sir Loadsocash'
And soaring with the Pope himself,
Over the rainbow of the world.

Amy Pippard (11)
Cove Junior School

THE TOWERING SUNFLOWER

The towering sunflower queen,
Inspires all the rest,
With her wonderful crown of gold,
Standing on a throne of green,
With lovely jewels all over,
That's what makes her the queen.
Her king is next to her,
With the Prince and Princess.
Their long thick stalk,
Holding them straight,
Above all the rest.

Hayley Hawthorne (10)
Guillemont Junior School

WATER

Water, water everywhere
It evaporates into the air
Twisting and turning
Slivering and sliding
Inside your body.
It keeps us alive
Day and night
And makes the streams
Bubble and flow.

Lewis Dodds (9) & Richard Songhurst (10)
Guillemont Junior School

A MILLENNIUM DREAM

I see the firing golden sparks,
Parachuting in the air
A special time of night has arrived
I wish I could sit on the moon
To see the dark blue sky
Stars sparkling above me
Painting pictures in my mind

Will my dream come true?

Matt Trotter (10)
Guillemont Junior School

THE FIGHTING TEMERAIRE (JMW TURNER 1775-1851)

The cool air whistles across my face and up through my hair,
My boat shaking, but only gently,
Complete and utter silence, apart from the gentle splash of oars nearby,
Under the sky's clouds versus the day's sun battle there is a subtle
      blue colour,
It is a beautiful orange haze followed by and dimly lit sun,
The gentle waves lapping my boat,
The nearly unnoticeable swaying of the river,
It is a paradise.

The houses at the side of the river,
Bustling with hundreds of people,
Hundreds of worlds,
Hundreds of lives,
The far off boats going off on long untold and unexplained voyages,
The sounds of far off shouts and laughs,
Drawn into the sighing of the sea,
The sea lit up with the vision of the ever-darkening sun,
It is a sight of pure joy.

A once great oak battleship,
Towed in as a prize of war,
A giant quietly humbled,
Once proud, now disabled,
Looks untouched, deeply wounded,
Misfit in a heavenly scene,
Dragged through perfect waters,
Greeted by friendly people,
Yet lonely,
In a paradise.

Mark Bond (11)
Guillemont Junior School

3

A MILLENNIUM DREAM

My millennium dream is for,
No more war along with violence,
Only hope and love in my world,
The hope and feel of something new
Is spreading through my bones.

The bolt of peace has thrown itself into the ocean,
Now it has splashed up on the shores of the Seychelles.
And vastly spreading towards Australia
And is slipping beyond
Will you make my dream come true?

The silvery lilac of the bolt of peace has done its job,
Now it's up to you -
Please make my dream come true.

Bethany Harris (10)
Guillemont Junior School

A MILLENNIUM DREAM

The sparkles in the sky have brightened up my dreams
There is an amazing leaping light in the dark grey sky
I dream I will meet S Club 7
Please make that dream come true
I wish I could do all the somersaults
And I wish that I could be in the circus.
What do you wish for?

Katy Bovington (10)
Guillemont Junior School

A MILLENNIUM DREAM

Fireworks leaping in the air gracefully whizzing
But then a great pop, it's gone.
My wish would be for all the rain to stop in Mozambique,
That more helicopters could be sent out.
How could we help?

If people would stop polluting our country
We could increase the number of animals.
Will it ever happen?

I wish war and violence would stop.
In Kosovo millions of people are homeless.
Will my dream come true?

Roni Adams (10)
Guillemont Junior School

WATER POEM

Water is the world,
There's rivers and elegant streams,
There's ice and boiled water,
My tears when I cry, my mum's wine,
I splash, I dive, I play all day.

There's pools and floods,
The rain and the puddles,
And don't forget the best of all,
My hot bubble baths!

Daniella Conway (11)
Guillemont Junior School

MY ELEGANT ROSE BUSH

In my back garden I have a luminous rose bush.
She is ridged, jagged, cerise and inspiring.
She stands in front of the wall.
She dreams of a soft look.

She clambers up the wall, as if she is lost.
She sparkles in the sun.
Soon she will die then come and grow beautiful next summer.
For now, withering while she takes her last breath.

Laura Holt (11)
Guillemont Junior School

THE ROSE

Rosie
Who is gentle, elegant and calming
Genus of a rose
Who is taller than your imagination
Who is as mighty as your hopes and dreams
And your strength to win
Who fears the sense of evil, the bad and the Devil
Resident of your soul

Freya Gibbs (9)
Guillemont Junior School

DRAGONFLY

D   arting dragonfly.
R   ushing in the reeds.
A   ttractive.
G   reen little dragonfly.
O   ften found roaming round a pond.
N   ever quite still.
F   eather light.
L   ove to watch it in flight.
MY little dragonfly.

Liam Tarry (11)
Guillemont Junior School

THE BUTTERFLY

I saw a butterfly, gracefully flutter by.
Through my window, it flew, like a dove,
Silently swooping through the trees.
Its bright wings looked like a roaring fire on fireworks' night.
It flew around my lamp attracted to the light,
I reached out to it and it flew away.

Samantha Barton (9)
Guillemont Junior School

IF

If you can listen to the teacher,
Whilst everyone around you is talking,
If you do your homework,
While your mates are outside playing,
If you can play nicely and do not start a fight,
You will be safe and not injured,
If your work gets copied,
You will know others don't understand.

If you eat all your lunch,
You will have enough strength to work all day,
If you remember your PE kit,
You will not have to sit on the side and watch,
If you listen to what you have to do and do your work,
You will not fall behind in different subjects.

If you can do all of these things,
You will be a successful person in life.

Stephanie Wright (10)
Kings Furlong Junior School

MY HANDS

M aking gigantic blocks of wood
Y oyo bobbing up and down like they should

H andstands falling side to side
A lways touching people's pride
N aughty hands look what you have done!
D id you break it? It's not fun!
S illy hands, don't do it again!

Charlie Harris (9)
Kings Furlong Junior School

IF

If you can concentrate in class while everybody else is talking,
If you can answer questions, even though you're not quite sure,
If you keep your eyes on the teacher, while the person next to you
      is talking,
If you can line up for assembly, when everybody is distracting you.

If you can sit down quietly even though you were desperate to speak,
If you can complete your work although your friend is really
      irritating you,
If you're good at all times even though you want to have fun in class,
If you can do work although your television is blasting out in the corner
      of the room,
If you can work carefully and everybody else can't write neatly,
If you can pay respect to all people while everyone else is
      being horrible,
You can be the most intelligent pupil ever.

Zoe Town (11)
Kings Furlong Junior School

CLARISSA

She is a sparkling diamond beaming in her presence.
A precious gem, dazzling with excitement.
She moves so swiftly, elegantly,
Like the gentle flow of a river,
Like a glistening swan that moves silently,
Skimming across the water,
Swooping high and low.
Her hair is as radiant as the sun,
Like crystal clear water, pure and clean.
Yes, she will always be there, especially for me!

Bethany Downham (10)
Kings Furlong Junior School

IF

If you can be lied about
Without having to lie,
If your wall has been desecrated
You can build it up again,
If you can be pushed around
Without having to push,
If you're playing fair
While others are playing dirty:

If you obey the rules
Even though elders don't,
If you can be polite and sensible
While others swear and fight,
If you can win the race
Without having to boast,
If you can achieve a goal
Even though others fail miserably;

If you can keep a secret
While others spill your thoughts,
If you can spend your money wisely
When others spend their money on sweets,
If you can solve a problem
Without others making it worse,
If you can achieve all this
You're sure to succeed in life.

Gabriella Slade (11)
Kings Furlong Junior School

THE MOON

The moon is a pale cheese
sailing in the sea of stars.

It is a milky golf ball
flying through the cold air.

The moon is a white torch
twisting in the wind.

It is a white snowball
crashing into frost.

The moon is a white fan
controlling all the wind.

It is a silver 10 pence piece
twirling in the air.

The moon is a silver pearl
glowing in the night.

Sarah-Jane Smith (9)
Kings Furlong Junior School

BETHANY

A little mouse she reminds me of.
When she's angry she never shows it.
When she is happy she reminds me of yellow
Because she's always bright and cheerful.
She's like a motorbike racing around.
She's clever and bright and intelligent and full of energy all day long.
She's like a fizzy drink and never flat.
Wherever life takes me she'll always be my friend.

Sara Keegan (11)
Kings Furlong Junior School

WHEN I AM 99

When I am 99, I shall not have mashed banana and beef stew,
I shall have machine gun pie.
I shall not drink milk and cocoa,
I shall drink tree juice.
I shall not spend my pension on a woolly hat and smart brown shoes,
I shall spend it on pop music.
I shall not read the paper and complete crosswords,
I shall shoot pig hearts.
I shall not wear long johns and black trousers,
I shall wear a Thunderbird outfit.
I shall not go to the shops and the kitchen for a cuppa,
I shall go to Fried Squiderife.
I shall not use a walking stick to travel,
I shall go by pogo stick!

I can't wait until I am 99!

Ben Hickey (8)
Kings Furlong Junior School

IF

If you can remember your books and work to the best of your ability
While people around you are being silly and wasting time.
If you can play a fair match and be a good player
While others are hacking and fouling.
If you can bring your homework on time and get a merit
While others do not bother to do it.
If you can always bring your PE kit on the right day
And have everything when some forget every time,
You will always be a star pupil.

Danny Jobling (11)
Kings Furlong Junior School

MY HANDS LET ME

M oving lots of Lego bricks
Y ogurt pots no use to me

H elp me write stories and poems
A lways there to help me lift
N ever stopping endless work
D oing things like wobbly handstands
S topping only at night

L ively and deafening when they clap
E ven when I'm writing this
T ypical hands always on the move

M onkey bars I love to swing
E ating my dinner my hands are in need

Maisie Hennem (8)
Kings Furlong Junior School

THE MOON

The moon is a round sugar lump dropped down from Heaven
It is a white boomerang thrown in the darkness of the sky
A drip of white paint dripped down by God
The silver top of a bottle cap dumped in the black sky ocean
It is an orphanage for the stars
A white Frisbee left on the marine shore
It will be your leader in the night
The moon is brother to the sun in the sky
They hang side by side

Jemma Rowlandson (10)
Kings Furlong Junior School

WHEN I AM 99

I shall not eat cereal for breakfast
    I shall have roast chicken and ice cream
I shall not drink coffee when I am thirsty
    I shall drink strawberry milkshake and Coke
I shall not spend my pension on bills
    I shall spend it on movies and chocolate
I shall not spend my time gardening
    I shall spend my time rollerblading and skateboarding
I shall not wear a jumper
    I shall wear snazzy ties and shorts
I shall not go to bingo
    I shall go bowling and go to Australia
I shall not travel around in a wheelchair
    I shall travel in a helicopter or a limo.

I can't wait until I am 99!

Jamie Andrews (8)
Kings Furlong Junior School

SIX WAYS OF LOOKING AT JANAY

She's a daffodil shining brightly in the sun.
She's a biscuit waiting to be eaten.
She is a diamond glistening endlessly.
She's a soft cushion that you can relax on.
She's the element of wind because what you say
Goes in one ear and straight out the other.
If she was a creature she would be
A monkey that scampers around for hours.
She is a mild curry on a hot plate.

Ross Greaves (11)
Kings Furlong Junior School

THE HEAVEN

The Heaven is a celestial world,
Scattered across the clouds.

It is an admirable place,
Resting amongst the sky.

It is a loving planet,
Watching over the Earth.

It is a joyful region,
Where the Gods hang out.

It is a peaceful area,
Where the good belong.

Remi Webb (10)
Kings Furlong Junior School

RAINBOW

The rainbow is a spill of oil,
From a car of Heaven.

The rainbow is a desire of hope,
From a corner of your only heart.

The ribbon of light flickers and is gone,
The rainbow is no more.

Sam White (9)
Kings Furlong Junior School

IF

If you can get all your own PE kit into your bag
without getting two left trainers.
If you can bring all your homework in at the right time
and have it all done every week, and every day.
If you can get out on the playground on time after a boring assembly
although it is cold and windy.
If you can put your hand up all lesson
and not mind if you do not get your say.
If you can do maths and not get all your two times table wrong
and not get upset about it.

Then you are a star pupil
and will get lots of tokens, my child.

Iesha Puddy & Rebecca Brannam (11)
Kings Furlong Junior School

WHAT IS THE MOON?

The moon is a silver coin
Jangling in a dark pocket.

It is a blue marble
Rolling down a steep marble run.

The moon is a grey wheel
Rolling around the long land.

It is a white clock
Ticking around the bold numbers.

The moon is a black tyre
Rolling down a steep hill.

Joshua Ness (8)
Kings Furlong Junior School

SIX WAYS OF LOOKING AT MY MUM

This person is like a kangaroo,
cuddly but fights if she needs to.
She is the element of water,
relaxing but can be deadly.
She is a rose with a thorn,
treat her delicately or she can hurt.
She is kind blue, sky blue, sea blue,
morning blue, bright eye blue.
She is milk; she is soft,
and helps in every way she can.
She is a teddy bear; cuddly,
soft, sweet and oh so loveable.
She is a cup of freshly squeezed orange juice,
in a diamond cup with a golden brim.

Elizabeth Hope (10)
Kings Furlong Junior School

SIX WAYS OF LOOKING AT MY MOTHER

She is as soft as a handmade sofa,
When she is angry she is like a fierce thunderstorm,
She can be like the sun shining bright
With nice refreshing clouds,
She is like a rose with a nice scent of smell,
She can be like a baby rabbit just waiting to be hugged,
She is like a nice refreshing glass of wine
Being poured into a gold crystal glass.

James Savine (11)
Kings Furlong Junior School

SIX WAYS OF LOOKING AT ALEX

He is a comfy sofa,
Who makes you relax.
He is the colourful dawn,
Welcoming in the day.
He is a pretty daisy,
Smiling at the sun.
He can be a glass of fizzy lemonade,
Fizzing like there's no tomorrow.
He is also little puppy dog,
Who follows you at your heels.
This person is the element of water,
Calm but can also be raging.
If he was a type of food,
He would be a sausage sizzling in a pan.
He dreams of a magical world,
Where there is no limit to his power.

Deborah Lock (11)
Kings Furlong Junior School

SIX WAYS OF LOOKING AT MY MUM

She's a relaxing computer chair,
which you can cuddle up in.
A beautiful sunrise in the morning you can enjoy.
She's a daisy that sways in the soft wind.
A sunny day that you could get burnt in.
A kitten playing in the gentle breeze with a leaf.
If she was a colour she would be pink for kind and softness.
She's a bar of chocolate, soft and sweet.
A warm jumper with a fluffy inside.
She's a can of Coke ready to explode.
She worries about getting all the jobs done and cooking all the meals.

Joanne Crowther (11)
Kings Furlong Junior School

IF

If you can go to school happily
without being worried about getting told off,
If you can do maths confidently
without getting angry about getting a sum wrong
If you can sit patiently in the most boring assembly
without talking to people
If you can play football safely at break
without getting the football smacked in your face
If you can sit quietly in wet play while everybody is shouting
If you can sing 'Songs of Praise' happily all morning
without getting a word wrong
If you can sit patiently through an English lesson

Yours is the merit point and everything its worth,
And - what is more - you'll be a star pupil, my child.

Alex Blunden & Jack Franzmann (11)
Kings Furlong Junior School

SIX WAYS OF LOOKING AT STEPH

She is like a white fluffy polar bear because they're soft but strong,
She is a firework worth one million pounds
Waiting to explode into many different colours,
Like a calm autumn day when the leaves are falling from the trees,
She is all the seasons rolled into one great year,
As fresh as spring, as sunny as summer,
And as calm as autumn, as sparkly as a winter's day,
If she was a food she would be a tropical fruit salad,
A banana waiting to be peeled, a zesty orange, a juicy mango
And put it all together, a taste of paradise,
A lovely warm coat on a cold, blustery winter day to keep me warm.

Samuel Marshall (10)
Kings Furlong Junior School

IF

If you can survive getting through the cloakroom
without getting battered to a pulp with bags and coats.
If you can get through the classroom door
without getting squashed after being battered with bags and coats.
If you are able to stay in class for two hours without falling asleep
while being taught by the most boring teacher *ever*.
If you can cope with going to assembly
and sitting on a hard floor with a ramrod straight back for hours on end.
If you can play football carefully without being smacked in the face
making you steam with rage and jump up and down wildly.
If you can listen carefully in an art lesson
while others around you are splashing each other with paints
which makes you feel so angry.
If you can sit through lunch
without getting splattered with lumpy mashed potato
which makes you feel like pulling your hair out.

Yours is the school, my son
and everyone that's it in
and what's more you'll survive school.

Katie Pilcher (10) & Joanne Donaldson (11)
Kings Furlong Junior School

SIX WAYS OF LOOKING AT JANAY

She's like a lovely bouncy bed.
She's like being in a swimming pool, just floating around.
She is like a sun making the whole world put a smile on their faces.
When it's a hot day, she's a comforting gust of wind.
When I'm bored, she livens me up like my cat.
She's like a cooling drink on a hot summer's day.

Jessica Hodgson (10)
Kings Furlong Junior School

SIX WAYS OF LOOKING AT STEPHANIE

She's a furry sofa making you feel relaxed when you sit down.
She's a baby cheetah whining as her mother leaves her.
She's a golden colour twinkling in the sun.
If she was a time she would be 7.00am on a nice hot day so she can see
      the sunrise.
She's a twinkling star, on a cold winter's night.
She's like a creamy pasta meal sizzling on a hot plate.

Katie Hailstone (10)
Kings Furlong Junior School

SIX WAYS OF LOOKING AT MY DAD

He's an old cupboard with rusting hinges,
He would be a bull with a red blanket over his eyes,
He would be a cold afternoon,
He is like a bubbling sherry which warms your belly,
He is the colour indigo, dark but mysterious,
He is the element wind that cools your neck,
If he was put in paradise he would still complain.

Michael Stainsby (10)
Kings Furlong Junior School

WHAT IS . . . A SNAIL?

It is a slimy monster leaving a silvery trail.
It is a traveller with a coloured house.
It is a slow car running out of petrol.
It is a copper penny rolling along.
It is a caterpillar track with a portable house.
It is a leaf-eating serpent munching slowly.

Laura Bourne (10)
North Waltham Primary School

WHAT IS . . . A FUNFAIR GROUND?

A funfair ground is lots of roller coasters
spinning round and round
the sound of screaming children bursts your ears
it's the smell of toffee apples
sticky and tasty
it's the rush of flying colours
bursting as if they were fireworks

Tina Wee (9)
North Waltham Primary School

WHAT IS . . . NEW YEAR?

New Year is a time for a new beginning,
A leaf waiting to be turned,
A turn along the road of life,
A closed door waiting to be opened,
A chance to make the bag we carry lighter,
A footpath gradually being used,
A new country being explored,
Another wave along the ocean.

Jordan Crame (10)
North Waltham Primary School

WHAT IS . . . A PUPPY?

A puppy is a small wad of wool,
It is a tiny ball of string,
It's a lion cub in its den,
It's an excited ball of fur,
It's a wet nose ready to sniff.

James Dodd (10)
North Waltham Primary School

WHAT IS . . . A GHOST?

A ghost is a haunting spirit sending a shiver down your spine,
It is a white sheet flying through the air,
It is an invisible sheet of paper that can walk through walls,
It is a cold gust of wind haunting you at night.

Natalie Ross (11)
North Waltham Primary School

WHAT IS . . . A GHOST?

It's a ragged old see-through sheet off a bed,
it's a death sway of terror,
it's a snowstorm,
it's a cold wintry snowstorm.

Andrew Suckling (10)
North Waltham Primary School

WHAT IS . . . A PUPPY?

A puppy is a bouncing spring with fur.
It is a slobbery monster waiting to pounce.
It is a stretchy bit of elastic lying untouched.
It is a raging rocket zooming wildly around.
It is a lion curled in its den.

James Atkin (10)
North Waltham Primary School

WHAT IS . . . A GHOST?

What is a ghost?
It is a ragged white sheet,
A big snowflake flying through the air.

A white sheet that sends a shiver down your spine,
A breeze of cold air that shoots through the air,
It is feeling when you walk through the graveyard.

Sophie Chivers (10)
North Waltham Primary School

WHAT IS . . . A GHOST?

It is a big snowball flying through the air, a wall-walking monster,
It is a terrifying monster's swaying sheet,
It is a frosty, cold gust of wind, running down your back,
A spinning storm terrorising the town.

Emily Cotterell (11)
North Waltham Primary School

WHAT IS . . . BACON?

A bacon strip fizzling and spitting in the pan.
It is all nice and tasty with a brown crispy tan.
It is the fiery flames of the sun crackling softly.
It is lovely and pink with a white outside.
It is a bacon butty which just finishes the touch.

Amie Clare (11)
North Waltham Primary School

WHAT IS . . . A GHOST?

A ghost is a shiver down my spine,
it is white gas to me.
It goes in houses and haunts everyone inside,
it gets out of its dead body and haunts the land.
It goes through walls.
Beware of the ghost.

Danny Whiteside (10)
North Waltham Primary School

WHAT IS . . . A PUPPY?

A puppy is a fluffy ball
It is a mad racing car
It is a jumping kangaroo
It is a cub lying in its den

Natalie Aldridge (10)
North Waltham Primary School

WHAT IS . . . A HEDGEHOG?

A hedgehog is a brown animal.
They are very wild.
It is a prickly bush made from thorns.
It is a pineapple but not to eat!
It is a brown cotton wool ball with sticks in.

Elaine Oliver (10)
North Waltham Primary School

WHAT IS . . . HAPPINESS?

Happiness is being with someone you care for.
It is the greatest feeling you can feel.
It is when you help someone.
It is when you feel excited.
It is when you are feeling kind.
It is when you are feeling friendly.

Iain Learmonth (10)
North Waltham Primary School

WHAT IS . . . THE MOON?

A twinkle in a dark forest changing colour hour by hour.
It is a white fingerprint on pages of black paper.
A speck of happiness outside the dimness.
Like a banana on a sea of dates.

Christopher Devonshire (11)
North Waltham Primary School

STORM

The thunder rolled like a giant boulder zooming down a mountain,
The lightning clashed its electric fork across the darkened sky,
The waves smashed the cliffs causing rock falls,
Wind howled like a hungry wolf,
The rain came tearing down pelting the ground with water.

Jack Hallett (10)
Oakridge Junior School

WHAT IS SPACE?

What is space?
A big open hole,
and there's no end to it.
What is space?

The things that fill space,
Venus and Mars,
Venus is my favourite,
God of peace and love.

Spinning, spinning,
the moon makes me dizzy,
while it's spinning,
around the Earth,
27 more days and there will be no moon at all.

Natasha McDonald (11)
Oakridge Junior School

MOONLIGHT

On a misty dark gloomy night,
I look out of my window into the dark scary sky.
I look above the shadowy trees and there's a light.
It is a beautiful bright light like a million crystals glinting in the sky.
I walk back to my bed and close my eyes.
I dream I am walking on the moon.

Leah Beeden (9) & Charlotte McCoy (10)
Oakridge Junior School

I LOVE THE MOON

I look up in the sky
And see
A round face looking down
On me
The round face is what people call
The moon
I don't want the morning to come
Because the moon will be going soon

But the morning comes
To my dismay
My mum makes me go out
And play
I go for my yummy
Delicious lunch
My friend gives me some sweets
Thanks a bunch

I see the moon glistening in
The sky
I wish I was a bird
So then I could fly
I love you moon
Don't go
I am going to be so lonely
Now you hang so low

Natalie Hine (10) & Holly Irving (11)
Oakridge Junior School

WHAT I SEE IN SPACE

I think I'm flying high at night,
I'm flying as fast as a meteorite,
I see Venus, Mars, Jupiter, Saturn, Pluto, Mercury,
I'm about to get flattened,
At half-past twelve I see a comet,
Raging fire coming from it.

When I was little, I thought the moon,
Was an everlasting pit of doom,
The full moon is my round belly,
And the gibbous moon is a piece of jelly,
The crescent moon is a fat banana,
The last quarter is half of my grandma.

I see rockets flying around in space,
I see an alien with a purple face,
I see millions of stars in the sky,
I see all the planets so high,
I see an asteroid zooming,
I see the sun booming.

Now I don't see rockets in space,
Or an alien with a purple face,
The full moon as a round belly,
Or a gibbous moon as some jelly,
Now I see space as space,
And nothing but space.

Nathan Steele (9)
Oakridge Junior School

THE MORNING

My alarm clock wakes me up at 7:15,
I get up, my hair is a mess,
I gel it down, it looks a bit better,
I get dressed into horrible school clothes
I go downstairs, my dad is feeding my cat
My mum's getting stressed because I'm so late up, it's 7:59
I get my breakfast, switch on the TV and watch Big Breakfast, it's 8:15
I go upstairs and clean my teeth, and wash my face
I pack my bag, my dad shouts up the stairs
I hear a slam downstairs
My dad is going to work
I say goodbye to mum
The house is silent.

Robert Dean (10)
Oakridge Junior School

WHAT I SEE IN THE MOON

What I see in the new moon is an endless dark pit.
What I see in a crescent moon is a lonely banana.
What I see in the first quarter is a half-eaten cake.
What I see in a gibbous moon is a big round tummy.
What I see in the full moon is a smile smiling back at me.

I see lots of things in the moon.
What do you see?

Stephen Coulston (9) & Daniel Washbourne (10)
Oakridge Junior School

SPACE

In space the moon lives
Above us in the sky,
The moon is shiny as a diamond,
Round as a cake
And sometimes a banana.
The stars are surrounding the moon like a prisoner.

I wish I could fly,
Fly to the moon
And fly to Mars
And I also thought Mercury is blue,
Mars is red,
Venus is yellow,
Jupiter is green
And Saturn is the darkest green in the world.

Clara-Louise Brightman (9)
Oakridge Junior School

MOON AND SPACE

The moon is as white as snow,
As cold as ice,
As hard as a rock,
As shady as a shadow,
All alone in the sky is the moon.

Space is wider than an elephant,
Taller than a giraffe,
As empty as a cardboard box,
As quiet as a mouse.

Veronica Craze (11)
Oakridge Junior School

SINGING PRACTISE

Oh no not another singing day
Everyone's squeak, squeak, squeak
I'm sitting there with my fingers in my ears

Squeak, squeak, squeak

Children's faces black and blue
Trying to get to the tune

Squeak, squeak, squeak

Help, help I'm screaming
Teacher my head's hitting the roof

Suddenly the piano stops
And no more
Squeak, squeak, squeak.

Jade Easton (10)
Oakridge Junior School

MOON'S PHASES

New moon, dark and dull,
Crescent moon, banana floating in the sky,
First quarter, half the moon has disappeared,
Gibbous moon, nearly complete,
Full moon, glow bright in the dark sky,
The moon keeps fading as phases pass
Dying . . .
Dying . . .
Dying . . .
Dead.

Joe Waller (11) & Billy Simons (10)
Oakridge Junior School

SINGING PRACTISE

La, la, la, la?
No that's not right, Rebecca higher!
La ,a ,a, a, a, a, stop right there
Start again . . .
Ah tew, yuk, there's snot everywhere
Can I got to the toilet please?
OK Alex, you may.
Jacob stop talking to Rebecca,
Right then, this is one of my favourites
silver trumpet.
I'm very sorry but it's break
But . . . but . . . you haven't finished
Miss Morrison!

Amy Best (10)
Oakridge Junior School

THE RAINBOW FISH

A shiny rainbow fish,
It lives in the deepest, purest blue sea,
Glittery, small, glinting,
Like a fast car,
Like wavy hair when it's curled,
I feel like I would love to see one,
I feel like I was one,
A shiny rainbow fish,
It reminds me of a disco.

Gemma Cobern (10)
Oakridge Junior School

THE MOON

The moon big, fat and bulgy, dark and light
The clouds go past the big, welcoming *moon!*
The bright stars crowd round the moon like a doughnut.
All the universe shining bright.

The sun shining on the moon like the day's sky,
Stars acting like rockets,
Very bright the universe is.

Jessica Bave (10)
Oakridge Junior School

THE NIGHT SKY

I see the moon high in the sky,
Shining brightly, bright like a bulb.
I wish I was the moon so I could see the world,
So I could see the animals and the fields down below.
I lay down in my bed with a dream in my head,
I dream on and on until I wake up.
I see the moon high in the sky.

Donna Marie Beeden (11)
Oakridge Junior School

SATURN

Saturn is huge
Beautiful butterscotch
Covers the sky.
Its rings
Some small, some big
Scatter across the sky.

Kirstie Ball (10)
Oakridge Junior School

IN MY BOX I WILL PLACE

In the box I will place

The tip of a devil's tail from the gloomy Hell,
the sparkling colours from the rainbow,
a twinkling white snowflake.

In the box I will place
A gentle splash from the blue sea,
a fluttering angel from God's kind maker,
the land of the green and blue Earth.

I will place in the box

The tip of a bat's tooth,
the shocking electricity from the black hole,
the smell of the scorching sunflower.

In the box I will place

A piece of the skunk's DNA,
the yellow beach with seagulls above,
a bat's black wing fluttering in the dark sky.

Sam Best (7)
Oakridge Junior School

MY DOG

My dog
My dog has been around for 13 years
Brown, black, white
She's as soft as a blanket wrapped round you
When I see her she makes me all tingly
When she's asleep she is so peaceful
Ssh, don't wake her, let her sleep.

Amy Butler (10)
Oakridge Junior School

IN MY BOX I WILL PLACE

In my box I will place,

a glittering snowman from the snow,
a shiny broomstick from up above,
and a yellow sparkling sun from the sky.

In my box I will place,

an enormous sandpit from a beach,
a fluttering angel from a palace,
and a freezing snowflake.

In my box I will place,

a fierce dragon from the underworld,
a rainbow in the colourful sky,
and a flying star in the blue sky.

Danielle Owen (8)
Oakridge Junior School

ZEBRA

The black and white zebra's big and tall
and its smooth skin rubbing on the tree.
The zebra's foot is big and black,
its face is thick as a branch,
his nose is big and grey
and its tail is as strong as a bamboo stick
and its eyes as white as clouds.

Craig Lapper (10)
Oakridge Junior School

IN THE BOX I WILL PLACE

In the box I will place

A tiny angel from the sky above,
A quivering snowman from the white snow,
And a fiery dragon from the Mediterranean.

In the box I will place

Some children watching the snowflakes melt,
A shooting star passing the moon,
A rainbow parrot talking to the sky.

My box is carved from glass, feather, snake skin and rubies,
My box is designed from crystals, gold, tinsel and diamonds.

I will fly to a dream world with my box,
Then I will time travel to the Roman times
Where I will become queen.

Sophie Irving (8)
Oakridge Junior School

COFFIN

A dirty coffin
Under the green grass
Dusty, smelly, old
Like an old door
Like a dirty box
It makes me feel dead
Like a quiet person asleep
A dirty coffin
Reminds me of death

Rebecca Clarkson (10)
Oakridge Junior School

I ONCE PUT IN THE BOX

I once put in the box

A glittering cat from a glittering moon,
A soft fluffy cloud from Heaven itself,
A golden lioness cub from Australia.

I once put in the box

A golden ring from Mars,
A sparkling rainbow from a magic clock,
The hot golden sun from outer space.

I once put in the box

A peckish monkey from Mars,
A cup of the water in the lakes of Canada,
And last of all, my teacher.

My box is designed out of glitter sparkle and tinsel.
My box has stars in the corners and snow round the edge.

I shall fly with my box over the Heaven gates to the angels,
Over the fluffy clouds and land back at home, sweet home
Where I will go up the stairs into my room and jump into my bed.

Mia Bradbury (9)
Oakridge Junior School

THE SHOOTING STAR

I look out my window
To see a shooting star
Flying across the night sky.
I start to wish that I could see it each night
I never can sleep
Because all I keep seeing is a bright light through my window.

I start to fall asleep
Dreaming I was in space
Never could stop looking at the shooting star.
The planets are going round and round
My head is spinning
Till I wake up

Claire Gray & Kayleigh Bull (10)
Oakridge Junior School

IN MY BOX I WILL PLACE

In my box I will place

a golden sweet puppy,
the shine of the sun,
an ice blue pond.

In my box I will place

a golden beautiful horse,
a sparkling angel,
a raindrop from Heaven.

In my box I will place

a cold icy snowflake,
the blue ocean,
and a bright star.

My box is designed from rainbow colours and snowy ice white.
My box has diamonds on the lid and secrets deep inside.

I will fly in my box to the bottom of the sea,
I can see fish, seaweed, starfish and boats.

Alice Taviner (8)
Oakridge Junior School

IN THE BOX I WILL PLACE

In the box I will place,

a parrot from the rainbow,
a cold tree from the South Pole,
the shining sun from the blue sky.

In the box I will place,

the biggest snake in Africa,
a very cold snowman,
a galleon from the South Sea.

My box is made out of silver and gold metal.
It is tied up by heavy chains.
I go diving with my box under the sea.
There's little and big fishes and a big blue whale.

Jack Gray (8)
Oakridge Junior School

THE RAINBOW

The bright colourful rainbow
Floats in the thin blue air
Bright, big, colourful
Like the bright shimmering sea
I feel small looking at it
I feel like I'm going under a bridge
The bright colourful rainbow
It makes me think of water.

Linzi Kynaston (11)
Oakridge Junior School

MY UNCLE'S DOG

My uncle's dog
At my uncle's house
Soft, fluffy, sweet
Like a ball of fluff
Like a horse running around the field
It makes me feel safe
Like a bear that's going to attack.
My uncle's dog
It makes me think of a special horse that won in the race.

Laura Graver (10)
Oakridge Junior School

THE SILKY DOLPHIN

The silky dolphin
Swimming in the bright blue sea,
Long, grey, beautiful,
Like a shiny glittery dress,
Like a squeaky mouse in water,
It makes me feel bouncy,
Like a ball bouncing on the ground,
The silky dolphin,
Reminds me of a fantastic holiday.

Jody Vockins (10)
Oakridge Junior School

THE MAGIC BOX

I will put in the box
An iridescent feather from a dancing peacock,
A sparkling angel from the glittering Heaven,
The silk from an elegant sweet smelling rose,

I will put in the box
The first pearly tooth of a baby,
A little spark from a snowflake,
A scale from a flameless dragon.

My box is designed from
Marble and petals and red rubies
With glamorous stars on the lid
And beautiful diamonds in the corners.

I shall fly in my box
On the wing of the dancing unicorn,
Across the cloudy heavens,
Then land in the centre of the silent moon.

Jade Evans (9)
Oakridge Junior School

A DOLPHIN

A bouncy dolphin
It is a silky dolphin
Smooth, wet, soft
It looks like a blue mermaid
It makes me feel very happy
Like I'm a smiley face
A dolphin reminds me of the colour blue

Alex Ariss (10)
Oakridge Junior School

THE MAGIC BOX

I will put in the box
A soft tickle from a royal mermaid,
The sweetest splash of honey from an elegant honeybee,
A first fiery breath from a Japanese dragon.

I will put in the box
A pearly cloud stroking the sun,
A spark from a shark's tooth,
A sway from a silk sari on a summer's evening.

My box is fashioned from ice and glitter and marble
With gold on the lid and promises in the corners.
Its hinges are made from a pterodactyl's toe joint.
I shall fly in my box through the arc of the heavens
And visit all my wishes and then land in all my dreams!

Lauren Ramsay (8)
Oakridge Junior School

THE MAGPIE

The magpie
In its nest
Feathery, colourful, agile
Like a fluffy cushion
Like a soaring plane
It makes me feel like I have wings
Like a black and white sign
The magpie
It makes me feel calm.

Ben Roberts (10)
Oakridge Junior School

THE MAGIC BOX

I will put in the box

A leap from a legendary dolphin,
The first flame from a golden dragon,
A sip of the swishing Atlantic.

I will put in the box

The eyes of a gleaming golden unicorn,
The icicle from a freezing glittering snowman,
The swish of a mermaid's tail.

My box is created from gems and marble and gold
With glittering stars on the lid and promises in the corners.
Its hinges are made from a legendary bird's wings.
I shall surf my box on a fire shooting rocket through the heavens
Then land on a legendary place
Where not even the legendary rocket has been.

Joshua Tuffs (9)
Oakridge Junior School

THE BED

The bed
In my bedroom
Comfy, springy, warm
It's like a soft fluffy cloud
Like a flurry of snow in winter
It makes me feel safe
Like a fluffy chicken
The bed
I feel like a leaf floating down a river.

Emma Faulkner (10)
Oakridge Junior School

THE MAGIC BOX

I will put in the box
a snowman with a melting body,
the first glance at the sizzling sun,
a roar from a lion creeping in the forest.

I will put in the box
a picture from an outstanding artist,
the first wobbly step from a baby,
a fossil found in Germany.

My box is fashioned from gold, silver and bronze
with ice on the lid and wishes in the corners.

Its hinges are the toe joints of a dinosaur.
I shall glide in my box over the moon
and land on Mars, the planet of green.

Elliott Buttle (8)
Oakridge Junior School

MY HORSE

It's a horse,
a beautiful horse standing in the field,
cuddly, beautiful and lovely,
like a little boy standing on his own,
it's the most precious thing in my whole life,
it's as if it's the most precious thing,
it's a horse,
it's the safest thing I've ever had.

Jonathan Hurst (10)
Oakridge Junior School

THE MAGIC BOX

I will put in the box
the first bud from a spring tree,
a tiny toe tickling a tiger,
the seven shimmering colours of the rainbow.

I will put in the box
many magnificent minerals,
a sweet word from a baby,
three gold wishes from a fairy.

My box is fashioned from pearls and gems and rubies
with glitter on the lid and memories in the corners.
Its hinges are the opening jaws of a tyrannosaurus.
I shall fly in my box to the wonderful world of wishes
in the pale blue sky
then land softly near the wishing well
in the light of the shining sun.

Amy Williams (7)
Oakridge Junior School

MY CAT

My cat
Is soft and cuddly
Furry, secretive, cute
Like a puff of snow in the air
As smooth as silk
Makes me feel completely empty
I feel as light as air
My cat
I feel as if I'm floating

Daniella Lupo (10)
Oakridge Junior School

IN THE BOX I'LL PLACE

I'll place in my box
A tree in the howling whistly wind,
The spark from a dragon's fiery breath,
The first glimpse of a platinum cup.

I'll place in my box
The sparkling lights of the first ray of the summer sun,
The first ever glow of the famous rainbow,
Receive a heavenly angel from clouds above.

My box is fashioned from diamonds,
Flying stars - multicoloured and platinum!
Locked with the best chains.

I shall time travel in my box to the great computer world!
While I'm in computer world I'll catch loads of Pokémon!
After that I'll play football with Man U!

Tom Roberts (8)
Oakridge Junior School

MY DOG

My dog,
At my house,
Soft, sweet and warm,
Like a ball of fur,
Like a playful baby running round the house,
It makes me feel safe,
Like a bear that's going to attack.
My dog,
It makes me think of a rabbit running round a field.

Charlotte Tipler (10)
Oakridge Junior School

CHRISTMAS TREE

I dropped onto my Christmas tree,

Rudolph with a dark grey nose,
Santa (like a Hollywood star) doing a great pose.

I rolled across my Christmas tree,

Santa growing out of his dungarees,
Rudolph catching reindeer fleas.

I threw onto my Christmas tree,

A pixie delivering presents,
Santa swapping Rudolph for a couple of pheasants.

I wrapped around my Christmas tree,

Santa keeping Stone Cold out of the ring for one minute,
Santa eating a pie with Rudolph's red nose in it.

Thomas Rawson (8)
Oakridge Junior School

MY DOG

My dog
At my house
Soft, sweet, smooth
Like a cuddly panda
Like a horse running through a field
It makes me feel warm
Like a soft bear
My dog
I feel safe and happy with him.

Lauren Brown (11)
Oakridge Junior School

IN THE BOX I WILL PLACE

In the box I will place:
A bursting galaxy of red dwarfs,
A thousand magical eclipses from FKC,
A fantasy moon from Pluto.

In the box I will place:
A warm wonderful bath full of bubbles,
Some tepid chicken burgers from the flaming sun,
And a million chocolate cakes.

In the box I will place:
Ten Game Boys with ten games,
Lots of gold pennies from lots of banks,
And a hundred sweets.

My box is created from strong silver metal
With coins on the lid and crystals at the bottom.
I shall time travel with my box into the future
Where I shall rescue a princess
Then have a banquet with the royal family
Before speeding back home again in time for tea.

David Smy (8)
Oakridge Junior School

MOON

I'm a fat pie,
I'm filled with cheese,
I'm now a small banana,
I'm an invisible ghost,
I'm really a Jaffa Cake,
I'm not any of these
I'm the . . . moon.

Daniel Brittain & Kris Ford (9)
Oakridge Junior School

IN MY BOX

In my box I will place
One of God's loving gifts from above,
A glittery star from the fresh sky,
One of Mary's favours for Jesus.

In my box I will place
The silkiest silk sari in the world,
A huge clump of sinking sand from India's desert,
A shivering feeling from a snowflake.

In my box I will place
My two friends Emma and Naomi
And I will put in my teacher.

My box is designed from gold, copper and glitter.
It has carved animals with glitter covering them.
My box has a gold ribbon round it
Its hinges have special secrets inside.
I will fly with my box to the North Pole
Where I will meet an elf and slide to the bottom of a rainbow.

Andrea Frewer (9)
Oakridge Junior School

HAIR

Hair
It sits on my head
Soft, smooth, straight
Like a bear's hair
Like a splodge of brown on my head
It makes me feel safe
Hair
I feel soft and happy now.

Chris Leonard (11)
Oakridge Junior School

50

THE CHRISTMAS TREE

I will hang on the Christmas tree
A dragon's tail rumbling
A baby robin stumbling
A Dalmatian beating a drum
The cat going 'Hum'.

I will roll on the Christmas tree
A tiger's knee
A purple flea
A mouse eating boar
My hamster going 'Roar'.

I will curl on the Christmas tree
A polar bear with footwear
My tree is full, I only need a bull.

Chloé Locatelli (8)
Oakridge Junior School

THE SUN

The sun
Boiling in space
Hot, fiery and burning brightly
Like an orange fresh off the tree
Like inside a mine burning for years
It makes me feel lucky to have it
Like a war
The sun
It makes me feel warm and comfortable.

Alex Hallett (9)
Oakridge Junior School

MY CAT TIGGER

My cat Tigger
Sleeps all over the place,
In a small case.
My cat Tigger
Has gold and black fur.
He purrs very quietly.
My cat Tigger
Is very cute,
He is the best,
He's good at making a mess.
My cat Tigger.

Billy Goddard (9)
Oakridge Junior School

MY CAT

My cat
lives at my house
fluffy, cuddly, soft
like a teddy bear in my bed.
I feel like a mum to her
I feel like a nanny as well.
My cat
I feel like falling asleep whenever I'm with her.

Zoe Brazier (11)
Oakridge Junior School

THE POLAR BEAR

The polar bear
At the South Pole
Big, fierce, furry
Like a giant
Like a warm coat
It makes me feel cold
Like an iceberg
The polar bear
I feel like I should take care of it.

Tiffany Mash (10)
Oakridge Junior School

MY HAMSTER

My hamster
At my house
Quick, swift, cuddly
Like a hairy sausage
Like a fluffy ball
Makes me feel happy
Like a hair ball
My hamster
I feel warm here

Joshua Nicholetts (9)
Oakridge Junior School

THE BEAR SCARE

The great bear
At the deep forest
Big, fierce, scary
Like a giant
Like a tall tower
It makes me feel scared
Like a crying baby
The great bear
I feel like hiding underneath my bed

Millie Wilson-Pearce (9)
Oakridge Junior School

THE CAT

The cat
At my house
Cute, soft, cuddly
Like a velvet cushion
Like a bumblebee
I feel like a giant
The cat
Makes me feel safe

Jade Emery (10)
Oakridge Junior School

MY CAT

My cat
At Mum's house
Soft, cuddly, smooth
Like a black panther
Like a big fluffy teddy
It makes me feel warm
Like a polar bear
My cat
I feel warm and safe with him.

Roxanne Boosey (10)
Oakridge Junior School

MY CAT

My cat,
At Dad's house,
Soft, smooth, cuddly,
Like a stripy tiger,
Like a fierce animal,
It makes me feel snuggly
Like a cushion,
My cat
I feel warm, cuddly and safe with him.

Kayleigh Ramsden (11)
Oakridge Junior School

My Computer

My wiry computer,
In my room,
Hard, firm, solid
Like a mechanical box
Locked in the monitor
Like a megabyte when I'm on it.
My wiry computer
I'm the spider crawling round the Internet.

Diana Farmer (10)
Oakridge Junior School

Chameleon

Slithery, crinkly across the jagged rocks,
Lies a small, silent chameleon with a massive pointed tail.

Colourful and camouflaged as he slithers,
Hiding and leaping in every rock.

His tongue as long as a giraffe's neck,
Munching and crunching as he devours leaves.

Sinead Wilson (9)
Oakridge Junior School

OLD GRANDADS

Old grandads are funny
They wear their coats
Even when it's sunny
They laugh at their own jokes
And call people 'folks'
They always watch telly,
And often eat jelly
(Because they've got no teeth!)
But when you're feeling down
They entertain you like a clown
They make you feel happy
And are never snappy!
They give you lots of sweets
To stuff up your cheeks
They can be very nice
And give us lots of good advice
Even when they're old and grey
They can still help us play all day
When you are not well
Amazing stories they will tell
Which are not true
But still stop you feeling so blue!
They're not so good at playing Lego
And this can be a pest!
But they always have a go
And always do their best.
Thank goodness for old grandads.

Justin Martin (8)
St Mark's CE Primary School, Farnborough

THE SEASONS

My name is Jack Winter,
And guess what? That's my favourite season!
I love to play in the crisp white snow,
Let's jump on the sledge, here we go!

Following straight after is spring,
That's my mum's least favourite!
She thinks it's the clean up season,
So we better tell her quick that it's not!

So now we are in summer,
That's Dad's favourite,
Because he gets to play cricket
Guess what? He's great at it!

Finally we get to autumn
Sophie loves this season.
She plays in the leaves,
And listens to hear them *crunch!*

Jack Winter (8)
St Mark's CE Primary School, Farnborough

TRULY SCRUMPTIOUS!

I adore chocolate,
It's always very yummy,
Flake and Twix and Mars bars
They're scrumptious in your tummy.

Chocolates of all colours,
I'll eat it dark or cream,
If my dad would let me,
I'd eat it with ice cream.

Whenever I have money,
Off to the shop I trot,
I buy as much as I can get,
And then I eat the lot!

Lydia Hemmings (9)
St Mark's CE Primary School, Farnborough

SPRING

When spring is here
New life is near
The birds start to sing
Oh, I do like spring!

The flowers start to bloom
The horse needs a groom
Out for a morning ride
Let's go for a little stride
Oh, I do like spring!

I can hear the ice cream bell
Everyone says, 'This tastes swell'
Ants crawling on the ground
Scampering all around
Oh, I do like spring!

A girl in a white dress
Making a daisy chain
Every day she does this
Again and again and again
Oh, I do like spring!

Lucy Norman-Walker (8)
St Mark's CE Primary School, Farnborough

MY INDIAN HOME

The river flowing gentle,
It glistens in the sun.
Play on the sand,
Elephants under palm trees,
A baby elephant having fun.

Running through the jungle,
Monkeys swinging around,
Tigers pawing on the ground,
Snakes slithering, we found.

We're swimming in the aqua blue,
Going underwater, look what I can see!
A coral reef, an angelfish, a stingray or two,
My friend the dolphin diving in and out.

My pet elephant and me,
Running in and out the coconut trees.

How I love my Indian home.

Frances Crossley (8)
St Mark's CE Primary School, Farnborough

WEATHER SIGHTS AND SOUNDS

Lying in bed wide awake while outside all around a storm
Wind howling like a lost dog
Thunder clashing like a gong being hit
While lightning lights the grey, black sky
Rain pattering on the roof
And big black clouds sail silently overhead

I wake up and look out of the window
Everything is covered with a thin frost
A pale sun is shining in the sky
Making the frost glimmer
And a gentle breeze is blowing the trees to and fro

Louise Holt (9)
St Mark's CE Primary School, Farnborough

OUR PLAY

Today was the day,
For our school play,
Everyone was watching me,
Everybody could see.

There were about sixty chairs,
When you're on stage everyone stares,
You look at your dad
He's a jolly lad.

At the end of the play,
I run and shout hurray,
Take the scrunchy off my head,
Run home, go straight to bed.

It is the night,
I turn off the light,
At that time I'm yawning,
I can definitely wait for the morning.

Chantal Dufour (9)
St Mark's CE Primary School, Farnborough

HUNNY BUNNY

My rabbit is called Hunny Bunny,
   Hunny Bunny is also very funny.
She plays with the curtains morning and night,
   And she loves to play and she never fights.
My rabbit sometimes lives in a hutch,
   And I love her very much.
She loves to eat kale,
   Then she goes very pale.
Hunny Bunny thumps her feet,
   And she loves to eat.
When she has a rest,
   She lies on her chest.

Lindsay Bicknell (8)
St Mark's CE Primary School, Farnborough

THE BEACH

I love the beach.
The sand tickling in between my toes.
I quite like the sea, freezing cold am I.
I like splashing and paddling.
But Mum always says
'Beware of the red crab's claws on your toe.'

I like the donkey rides.
Be careful not to slip off.
I like eating ice cream in the sunset.
And best of all I like going home
And dreaming of my exciting day.

Emily Ainge (9)
St Mark's CE Primary School, Farnborough

PETS

I take my dog for a walk
He rolls on the green tickling grass
I find my dog from under a bush
He has a pile of glass stuck in his paw
I take him to a vet
She pulls out the dirty glass
And puts a cotton bandage on his white furry leg
We go home and sit by the warm popping fire
He bites his bone
Later we go up to bed
He sits sighing by my head
We must take more care next time

Hannah Maley (8)
St Mark's CE Primary School, Farnborough

STEAM TRAIN

I went on a steam train
It huffed and puffed and sounded like a cat sleeping
The man gave me some Coke
It made me feel sick
I wanted home
I missed my father
I was very hungry
The man had gone

Daniel Maltwood (8)
St Mark's CE Primary School, Farnborough

DON'T BE SAD BECAUSE I AM MAD

Don't be sad
Because I am mad
I can make you smile
Don't be cross
I can get you a friend soon as poss.

Don't be sad
Because I am mad
I can make you smile
Don't run
Don't cry
You should get some comfort and smile

Don't be sad
Because I am mad
You should laugh
Not frown
A friend will be next to you in a while

Don't be sad
Because I am mad
You can laugh sometimes
Don't get cross
I can make you laugh
Soon as poss
    Ha, ha, ha
Told you I can make you laugh soon as poss

Tara Farrer (10)
St Neot's School, Hook

TECHNOLOGY

The phones are ringing,
Buzzers are buzzing,
The planes are screeching,
Speakers are going mad,
Radars are going zip, zip,
Remote control cars are zooming around,
Tanks roar.

But the birds still sing.

Still the buzzing goes on,
As well as the noise,
The radiators click,
The exhausts from cars stinks,
All the building going on,
People screaming,
And the big rocket takes off,
Boom, crash, bang.

But the birds still sing.

And they don't stop.

But technology goes on.

Jonathan McMillan (8)
St Neot's School, Hook

THE KILL

Trudging through the long grass, crisp with the fresh day.
Mist hanging suspended like saliva from a dog's mouth.
The game, silent, motionless. Nothing stirs.
The boggy land is dark, still.
The silence makes you feel it is going to grab you.
My boots patter across the bridge like rain.
There a bushy hedge, crying out to be used to hide in.
The wind makes it look like an over-stuffed turkey.
Rustling wind and bush hedge, my only camouflage.
There the soft beating of the wings . . .
Gun leaps smoothly to my shoulder,
The hammer falls like a woodpecker attacking a tree.
The bird, once so marvellous in its flight,
A crumpled,
Bunch of feathers,
Bloodstained,
Dead.

George Goddard (11)
St Neot's School, Hook

SHARK POEM

I saw a great white shark,
It chased me through the waves,
I swam for the beach,
But ended up in the caves.

The shark watched and waited,
And saw me swimming fast,
It caught me and bit me,
How long will I last?

Ben Dearden (7)
St Neot's School, Hook

EAT UP

Chocolate cake and strawberry jelly,
Really quite fattening, gives you a belly,
Toffee, chocolate and carrot cake,
Toffee pudding with a chocolate flake,
Blueberries, blackberries and raspberries with cream,
This is food you get in your dream.
Pink, red and blue lollipops,
Save up your money and get down to those shops.
Victoria sponge and yellow custard,
Sizzling brown sausages served with mustard,
Salty crisps and yellow popcorn,
Switch on the music and party till dawn.
Creamy cakes with cherries on top,
Lemonade and strawberry pop,
Vanilla ice cream and sugary shortbread,
That's enough for one meal, I'm going to bed!

Emily Olsen (11)
St Neot's School, Hook

HAIKU POEMS

The rabbit hopped fast.
He hopped into bright sunlight.
He enjoyed the sun.

The snake slithered round.
With no legs he crawled quickly.
Down, down, down and down.

The shark swam around,
To the bottom of the sea.
His fin swirling round.

Samuel Wikinson (9)
St Neot's School, Hook

THE DEADLY TOURNAMENT

Stormy, out in a giant city in space.
The Tournament looms over it.
Darkness forms a shadow of fear.
You are once again, under threat of death.

Fire rises around you! You're afraid!
You're gonna die! Fear!
You want help! Mummy can't save you now!
The heat rushes towards you! Pain!

The flames blaze away at you. But wait . . .
Cool air . . . water! Escape quickly!
Your team . . . their organs . . . ripped to pieces along the floor!
Avenge them now. Rip up the other team cruelly!

They're attacking you. One down. His blood flies.
Razors now. Duck! Dodge! Shoot! There goes another one.
His brain nauseously shoots past you! Shoot to kill!
Fear! Death! Night! Cold! War! Pain!
It's like the Grim Reaper, gently tapping on your shoulder.
   In the battlefield . . .

Lawrence Richards (11)
St Neot's School, Hook

THE WATERFALL

Splashes of dazzling blue water twinkling, spraying everywhere,
The water crashing and smacking against the pool.
Cascades cracking the water's mirror,
Blasting down at whizzing speed.
The pool brimful, nearly bursting its banks.
The water glistening in the sun.
Kids having loads of fun.

The waters collide at tremendous speed,
Ferocious and ravening noise all around.
Little rock pools overbrim, people staring into them in the sun,
Fast and lively rivulets spill and sprawl,
Ripples break out in the pool,
People having loads of fun.
Bam!
The torrents roar!

Thomas Reeves (10)
St Neot's School, Hook

LABYRINTH

Deep down in the labyrinth
In the cold and dank
With slime on the walls that really stank,
There was an unspeakable terror
Down there in the gloom,
And if you went down there
You'd meet your *doom!*
For there waited a monster
With razor-sharp teeth
And claws
And horns
And spikes on its tail like barbs or thorns.
If with its claws it gave you one slash
Then you'd be dead on the floor in a flash.
I wouldn't go in there unless you have a cord
Or a reel of string to tie to the door
'Cause without one of those you won't find your way out,
However much you scream or shout.
You'd be trapped down there forever
Condemned never to see the outside world. Ever!

Jamie Dinham (11)
St Neot's School, Hook

TELL ME A STORY ABOUT . . .

Tell me a story about girl a with long golden hair
And lips of the reddest rose
Or a story about a prince who is on a mission to find a bride,
But doesn't know the secrets deep inside.

Tell me a story about fairies dancing upon the flowers,
Making daisy chains and making dresses out of rose petals.
Or maybe a tale that comes from under the sea
About mermaids and pearls and sunken ships.

Or maybe a tale about unicorns dancing around in another land.
Or a tale about wizards making potions and spells.
Or a story about the Milky Way, stars, moon and planets far away.

I will search for a story high and low
And ask people from every corner of the Earth and say

'Tell me a story about . . .'

Eloise Riddle (11)
St Neot's School, Hook

FIRE POEM

The fire is crackling bright, red-hot,
Glittering in the freezing winter sun.
Sparks fly, glazing hot,
Yellow, red, orange.
The smoke is blown for miles and miles
While the blazing apple log scents the night.
The warmth is so warm, the fire so bright,
As if a light is on.
The fire burns warm and bright,
Long, long into the winter's night.

Charlotte Tongue (10)
St Neot's School, Hook

THE BATTLEFIELD

Men emerging from the trenches.
Crawling towards enemy lines.
Everything silent.
The occasional plane.
The sudden sound of a machine gun.
The whine of bullets overhead.
The crunch of barbed wire being cut.
The men take the enemy trench.
Killing everyone in their sleep,
Silently gassing them,
Their skins wrinkle.
Blood!
'Can't see!'
'Mustard gas!'
Shot in the head -
Everyone dead!

James Wilkins (11)
St Neot's School, Hook

MY FAMILY

I love my family
So dearly.
I love them because
They are kind and generous.
They play with me,
I get piggy backs.
They love me,
So clearly,
So dearly.

Catherine Raggett (8)
St Neot's School, Hook

RIPPLES IN THE SEA

The sea is calm, the sea is gentle, the sea is quiet.
The ripples ripple small, big, bigger, *whoosh!*
Whales and seals and dolphins, leap into the air,
A huge tidal wave rains shells and crabs,
The rock pools have trapped sand and salt and pebbles,
On top of all the boulders sits a pretty house,
It shows ships the way, why it's the big lighthouse.
Seagulls dip and dive catching fish and such,
While the wind and rain rages on,
The fish jump and swim away,
The beach becomes a lake,
Suddenly the sun breaks through the jet-black sky,
Sending the darkness spinning over the horizon,
The ripples ripple, small, big, bigger,
Who knows what they will bring this time?

Catherine O'Farrell (10)
St Neot's School, Hook

SWEDEN

S   nowing in the winter.
W   et in the autumn.
E   veryone's happy.
D   ad's at work.
E   very single person is warm.
N   ow the summer, nice and warm.

S   now, I love snow.
N   ice and fluffy snow.
O   n the windows.
W   indy and cold.

Emilie Bergström (8)
St Neot's School, Hook

SNOW POEM

The pearl white snow lightly falls,
Leaving a crisp crust,
I look out of the window and see a blanket of snow,
It's hanging off the trees like icicles,
There, in it, is a deep footprint,
It looks like cotton wool,
The pond has mysteriously turned to ice,
A chilly breeze rattles my window,
Slip marks are faint in the snow,
I touch it and my hand turns like stone,
It drips off branches, turning to water,
The lamplight shines dimly in the moonlight,
My vision . . .

Sophie Farelly (10)
St Neot's School, Hook

THE STREET OF CLUB JUGGLERS

The street laughs, cheers and laughs again,
The jugglers make those laughs and cheers,
Whether it's bright or dull.

It might as well be called Laughter Street,
For it's the brightest around,
It might be up ladders or riding around on unicycles.

But the almighty balls and bats are always there,
Making that amazing feeling of joy.

The crowds don't know why,
But they enjoy the fun,
Bright or dull.

Thomas Smart (10)
St Neot's School, Hook

THE WEDDING

After the wedding she plays hide and seek
and tells the bridesmaid not to peek.
I bet the bride regrets it now she's stuck in the carved oak box.
It looks like it contains a treasure,
gold, silver and more,
but anyone who opens it won't find that at all.
From the darkest corner to the brightest window,
she haunts everywhere; she knows where you go.
Walking down the garden path
you will smell lilies as you pass,
for the sweet white plant was the wedding flower.
If you dare go up the spiral stairs to see the pale white face
you will surely get pushed back down again
by the White Spirit of the house.

Rebecca Harman (10)
St Neot's School, Hook

FRIENDS

When you've had a fight and you've been left alone,
Your friends have gone into a gang against you.
Wishing you could be friends again but you are too shy to ask.
Sitting there in darkness, wishing to be bold and ask,
But being pushed away.
Remembering the old memories and trying not to cry,
Trying to get them out of your mind.
Thinking of the past few days, and of what went wrong today.
Then you go over to them and slowly say in a shaky voice,
'I am sorry' and give them a great big hug.

Rebecca McNutt (10)
St Peter's CE Junior School, Farnborough

TEN TALL PINE TREES

Ten tall trees which were pine
'Barrels,' said the farmer, then there were nine.

Nine tall pine trees, blowing to the gate
'Floorboards,' cried King Henry, then there were eight.

Eight tall pine trees, pointing up to Heaven
'Paper,' said the bookmaker, then there were seven.

Seven tall pine trees, all in a fix
'Firewood,' said the cook, then there were six.

Six tall pine trees, blowing near a hive
'Chairs,' said the Queen, then there were five.

Five tall pine trees, who grew near the moor
'Tables,' said the woodcutter, then there were four.

Four tall pine trees, shading me
'Beds,' said the maid, then there were three.

Three tall pine trees, growing straight and true
'Cupboards,' said the carpenter, then there were two.

Two tall pine trees, glistening in the sun
'Toys,' said the toymaker, then there was one.

One tall pine tree, left alone for years
'Pruning,' said the gardener, so out came the shears.

Ha! Ha!

Rebecca Attridge (7)
St Peter's CE Junior School, Farnborough

MOUSE

There's a mouse under my stairs,
He scurries out and in.
My mum will go ballistic,
If she knows he's in the bin.

I don't know what his name is,
Anyway, I call him Fred,
Cos when he's really scared,
He hides under my bed.

He plays inside my doll's house,
He's really having fun.
Oh no! He's falling off the chair,
Quick, I'd better run.

I laid him on the bed,
He bounced up and down.
I think that he's OK,
But he's giving me a frown.

I let him in the garden,
He ran around like mad.
Then he found another mouse.
It made me really sad.
(No happy!)

Now I have two friends to play with,
They scurry out and in.
Mum still doesn't know,
Guess what? They're hiding in the bin!

Sarah Dunford (8)
St Peter's CE Junior School, Farnborough

GOD'S CREATION

God made an Earth covered with land
Some of it was green and some of it was sand
He put in blue and green clear seas
And on the land different trees.

Next He made the night and day
The moon, the stars and the sun's hot ray
He made the trees, plants and flowers
Then the clouds which gave them showers.

Then He made the living things
Some with legs and some with wings
In the sea He put dolphins and whales
And on the earth slugs and snails.

Next He made the bugs and spiders
Some needed to be good hiders
He made the butterflies and bees
Then all the different countries.

Then He made the birds and ducks
And the world was filled with songs and clucks
He made the cows, the pigs, the hens
He made the robins and the wrens.

Finally He made me and you
And once on it what did we do?
We polluted the clear blue sky
Which caused the animals to die.

Abigail Burch (11)
St Peter's CE Junior School, Farnborough

STORM

The start of a storm
Is the pitter-patter of rain
Then as it gets harder
The hail starts to fall
As the thunder and lightning
Flash and boom
In the gloomy, grey sky
And a great gust of wind
Blows the trees to the side
As they curve over you
And shadow you in darkness
As it gets to the end
The sun has defeated the storm
As the cloud and mist from the sky
Fade away and the sun shines into the day.

Alexandra Tulip (10)
St Peter's CE Junior School, Farnborough

WINTER

I was as cold as
The frozen frost in Iceland
Winter, cold as the bottom of the ocean
With frozen, dull leaves falling from grey, pale skies
and
Silver clouds,
Damp rain and puddles,
Frosty snow and shivering winds
Travel to my mind.

George Barker (8)
St Peter's CE Junior School, Farnborough

MY DAD

Dad, Dad you are the best,
Honestly you can beat the rest,
You are kind and you play with me,
Horrible, well, occasionally.

I'd like to tell you something, Dad,
Hopefully this won't make you mad,
I thought this poem up for you,
While I was sitting on the loo.
It was fun,
And after I was going to have a bun,
But I changed my mind.

Christmas is a time I like to see,
You camcording joyfully,
Dad, I will now call you 'The great',
And I hope you appreciate,
This poem I wrote for you,
Yes, I do!

Christopher Wenham (9)
St Peter's CE Junior School, Farnborough

DOLPHIN

D iving in the waves,
O ver and over again.
L olloping up, down and all around,
P ouncing like a dog.
H ippity, hoppity,
I n and out of the waves.
N ow it is time to rest, rest, rest . . .

Emma Browne (9)
St Peter's CE Junior School, Farnborough

A WINTER POEM

Winter is cold and icy.
Winter is pale and bare.
Winter is freezing and blustery.
Winter is snow and rain.
Winter is grey and wet.
Winter is silver and foggy,
Just like a silver and beautiful tree.
Winter is dull and damp
Like a chilly and horrible prison.
Winter is a polar bear
White and soft.
Winter has a beautiful glow
Of silver and light grey.
Winter makes my toes really cold and numb.
Winter is foggy and makes me tremble.
Winter has hailstones and snowballs.
Winter has a glistening white frozen lake,
Easy enough to skate on.
Winter is all these wonderful things,
That's why I love winter!

Charlotte Byrne (8)
St Peter's CE Junior School, Farnborough

WINTER POEM

I was as cold as the Antarctic,
When the icy snow rained down on us,
The bare, black branches shivered in the cold,
When the snow rained down on us.

I was as cold as the Antarctic,
When the blustery wind froze us,
The foggy, frozen frogs croaked,
When the wind froze us.

Alan Phelan (9)
St Peter's CE Junior School, Farnborough

THE ALIEN THAT CAME TO TOWN!

The alien is coming
He's heading our way,
He landed on the planet Earth
Only yesterday!
He ran straight across the road
And stopped all the cars,
Does he come from Venus,
Jupiter or Mars?
Better be careful,
Better stand aside,
You can see the alien's teeth
When he opens his mouth wide!
He's running down the street
Better shut your doors,
You don't want to get caught
By his thousands of claws!
The whole town is wrecked
The alien goes away,
That's the last time the town
Has an alien to stay!

Rebekah Williams (9)
St Peter's CE Junior School, Farnborough

IMAGINATION

There is a special place somewhere,
Somewhere, where princes fight dragons,
Where unicorns fly through the night,
Where kings and queens go to wonderful balls.

There is a special place somewhere,
Somewhere, where animals talk,
Where trees walk around,
Where birds go tweet, tweet in the park.

There is a special place somewhere,
Somewhere, where witches brew potions in cauldrons,
Where genies grant three wishes,
Where people turn into frogs.

There is a special place somewhere,
Somewhere, where these things come from.
Somewhere to think alone.
Somewhere deep in my imagination!

Rebecca Cagney (11)
St Peter's CE Junior School, Farnborough

RED

Red is blood
When it's hurtling through the body
Red is an apple
All crunchy and ripe
Red is a rose
Scented and bright
Red is fire
Blazing and crackling

Kate Stallard (8)
St Peter's CE Junior School, Farnborough

ANGER

Anger is a fire
That never stops burning
Through the heart and into the brain.
It feels like
I have to do something bad
I will kill, kill, try to kill anger
My face is going red
Steam is coming from my ears
I am cross
Anger is the red
Of killing and death
And a door that never opens to happiness
Anger is bad.

Charlotte Johnson (9)
St Peter's CE Junior School, Farnborough

SADNESS

Sadness is . . .
When you're being treated like you're not there.

Sadness is . . .
When clouds go over the blue, clear sky.

Sadness is . . .
When you feel like a dog that's lost its way home.

Sadness is . . .
When your closest friend dies
and you feel like bullets have been shot into you.

My heart is full of sadness.

James Cagney (9)
St Peter's CE Junior School, Farnborough

THE MAGIC BOX

I will put in the box,
A small breeze on soft velvet skin,
The scale of a sacred snake,
A mosaic made from grains of sand.

I will put in the box,
The bounce of a bed,
A melting snowflake
And a newborn chick.

I will put in the box,
The shine of a star,
A jungle's exotic plants,
The matter of time.

I will dream in my box
Of all different wonders
On the edge of the universe,
Drifting and floating through nothing.

Peter Marron (10)
St Peter's CE Junior School, Farnborough

WINTER

The silver, shivering snow lay on the ground
I was as cold as an igloo house on a dull grey day
A foggy, frozen frost drifted through the air
Like a smooth, flying bird
A trembling wind sailed through my head
Chilly dull snowflakes rained on the dark, dull street.

Samuel Jones (8)
St Peter's CE Junior School, Farnborough

HOLLY BERRIES

Step into the wood
and smell holly berry,
It'll make you alive
and light as a cherry.

It's a wonderful smell,
the holly berry.
It'll make you alight
and feel merry.

Now this poem
must come to an end.
It can't go on forever,
my dear, dear friend.

Bryna Godar (8)
St Peter's CE Junior School, Farnborough

WINTER

Wet, white snow glittering on the ground,
Snowball fighting,
Snowflakes falling,
Snowmen built, melted by the sun,
Excited children in the snow,
Children as cold as the bottom of the ocean,
Children trembling in the snow,
Silver, white fog in the air,
Frozen ice on the lakes,
Freezing icicles falling to the snowy floor.

Donna Quincey (8)
St Peter's CE Junior School, Farnborough

WINTER

Winter is cold.
Winter is white.
Winter is cold with blustery winds.
Winter's black branches from the trees
Are filled with snow on top.
Winter is the time,
When snowflakes fall.
Winter is when snow
On the rooftops of houses
Is like icy cold mountains.

Oliver Johnston (8)
St Peter's CE Junior School, Farnborough

POEM ABOUT ARSENAL

Arsenal, Arsenal hear them roar,
Arsenal, Arsenal let's hear more.
Here comes Man U dragging on the floor,
And here comes Arsenal winning the war.
Let's sit down and watch the game,
I put a bet on that Arsenal win the game.

There goes Bergkamp running down the wing,
There goes Adams into the box.
Let's watch this, there goes a *goal!*
What a shot, we won the lot!

Rikki Brittin (10)
South Farnborough Junior School

MY COMPUTER

My computer
Is the best.
My brother is always on it,
He is a pest.

My computer,
Has got a printer.
I can't go on it,
Because I've got a splinter.

My computer,
Has got a spell check.
It is clever,
Because it's very hi-tech.

My computer,
Has got a wordpad.
It broke down last month,
Now I am very sad.

My computer,
Has got a keyboard.
The reason why it broke,
Is that my mum chopped it with a sword.

My computer,
Has got the Internet.
My computer is so good,
It is like an electronic pet.

Sam Pool (10)
South Farnborough Junior School

COOL DUDE

There once was a boy called Daniel
His mum thought he was a brat
Every day he ran around the house
Tearing up the cat.

When he went to his friends one day
All his friends were cool
He said, 'I've made a motto,
We all hate school!'

When he went to the park the next day
He met his teacher there
He asked her, 'What are you doing here
And what's that spider in your hair?'

The teacher looked straight after that
And this is what she said,
'I was catching spiders with a net
Down in my new garden shed.'

When his mate came round for tea
He said, 'Hello,' to Auntie Pam
And they grabbed
A slice of bread and jam.

The next day when he went round Sam's
They said they'd play on the computer
But then they decided they'd better
Play on his brand new scooter.

They did their homework together
The teacher remarked,
'It's better than ever
Are you sure you didn't do it together?'

When he went on the coach
To leave for his school trip
It was pouring down with rain
He pierced a hole in the roof
The rain trickled in - drip, drip, drip.

Sophie shouted out,
'Look what Daniel's done, Miss!'
The teacher turned around
And gave a loud *hiss.*

I hope you're glad
He's not your brother
All he'll do
Is wind up your mother!

Rhiannon Harrison (9)
South Farnborough Junior School

SPACE

Space is big
Space is black
Space is cold

Stars are bright
Stars are small
Stars are light

Planets are dots of colour
Planets are round
Planets are small

William Sterry (9)
South Farnborough Junior School

BEES

I hear the buzz of a bee,
I cannot see it in the tree.
Bees have yellow and black stripes,
They are thin and long, just like pipes.

I hear the buzz of a bee,
Where it is I cannot see.
It is collecting nectar from a flower,
Is it waiting for a shower?

I hear the buzz of a bee,
Is it coming to sting me?
It will make honey,
While we make money.

I hear the buzz of a bee,
While I sit and drink my tea,
I see its wings,
Like taking off with springs!

I hear the buzz of a bee,
As it sits watching thee.
It is bigger than a flea,
And used much more usefully.

Jessica Castle (10)
South Farnborough Junior School

MY CATS

I have a cat called Beamish,
He makes me very squeamish,
He brings home dead mice,
Which isn't very nice,
But I still love my cat called Beamish.

My other cat called Reg,
He likes to sleep on the edge,
Sofa or chair,
He doesn't really care,
That's my cat called Reg.

Chantal Comeau (10)
South Farnborough Junior School

BEST DAY IN THE USA

D isneyland, here we come
I 'm so excited, it's going to be fun
S uitcases packed, ready to fly
N ot long till the plane zooms up in the sky
E ventually we land in the USA
Y oung people all around me saying, 'Have a nice day.'
L ooking and listening for Disney characters in the land
A utograph book read in my hand
N ext it's off to see a show
D azzling acrobats all in a row

F antastic rides to amaze and delight
L ike the Haunted House which gave me a fright
O ccasionally we stop to eat
R esting our bones and tired feet
I t's 3 o'clock, time for the band
D ancing together hand in hand
A n amazing day in the USA.

Avril Judge (10)
South Farnborough Junior School

MY GREAT SEA ADVENTURE

I'm off on a great sea voyage
To an island off the barrier reef.
I'm really looking forward to it.
I hope we don't get much grief.

The captain is my dad
He thinks I'll do OK.
This is my first sea voyage
I hope things go the right way.

Our mates are one-eyed Norm,
Bob Taylor and John Moore.
They have sailed with my father
On many voyages before.

Our ship is tall
With huge white sails.
Old Jake was down below
Making a dish with sausages and ale.

The weather blew up a stormy night.
It tossed and turned the boat
It gave me such a fright.
I was in my bed listening to the storm
But who came in? Old one-eyed Norm!

He is such a friendly chap.
Also the one who found the treasure map.
He talked to me about his adventures on the sea.
He also laughed and smiled with me.

We got there in the morning
I heard the captain calling,
'Aiyee, me mateys, we've found the gold,
Let's go home before we grow old.'

Emma Haynes (11)
South Farnborough Junior School

JOURNEY TO OUTER SPACE

I've always wanted to be an astronaut
And get blasted into space,
See an alien and watch an astro race.
This was my dream.

I was awakened by a shaking of my bed,
As I opened my eyes I realised I wasn't in it.
I was in a harness that was tightly fit,
Where am I?

The vehicle I was in started lifting itself off the ground,
Was I still dreaming?
I tried screaming,
But nothing came out.

I had calmed down now,
But then there was a loud thump,
And where I had hit my head there was a large bump.
We have landed on the moon!

I put on a funny suit and went outside.
There was a crater I didn't see,
And I tripped over it unluckily.
I started to fall but never stopped.

But when I did land it was on my bed.

Samantha Warner (11)
South Farnborough Junior School

AT THE BEACH

As I sit upon the beach
And gaze out to the sea,
And sink my teeth into my peach,
As part of my picnic tea.

I wonder about the little waves
Lapping on the sand.
Have they travelled many days
Before arriving on our land?

Upon the mud the boats just sleep,
Not wearing any wellies,
Waiting for the tide to creep,
As crabs tickle their bellies.

I wish I could live near the sand,
It is always so much fun.
Sadly I live far inland,
So cannot often come!

Becky Stamp (9)
South Farnborough Junior School

GONE AGAIN

With a toss of her head
She gallops past
Her mane and tail flowing behind her
In the open wind.
She stops and dips her head towards the rising river
Then runs and is gone again.
She canters between the trees and stable
To nibble the grass
Then with a start is gone again.

Mercedes Bennett (10)
South Farnborough Junior School

NORTH SEA VOYAGE

I visited Staithes by the sea,
I was offered a voyage by a fisherman for free.

We dragged the nets for a day or two,
We caught one cod then two.

But then we realised that we were through,
For there is no more cod, either for me nor you.

Back to the harbour we did chug,
With two fishes in the tub.

Calling out to the people on shore,
There will be no fish forever more.

What else do we eat instead of fish?
We'll have to think of another dish.

Cooking cod was my favourite thing to do,
Just so my mum didn't make me cook Irish stew.

Sophie Cush (11)
South Farnborough Junior School

THE ROSE

Gracefully opening to disclose,
Richest treasured flower that grows.

Fold on fold of ruby red,
Lying together in a gardener's bed.

Symbol of everlasting love,
Beautiful as the whitest dove.

Yolanda Wynn (9)
South Farnborough Junior School

WAR

It is bleak, powerful, forsaken.
War.
It is black, grey, deadly.
War.
It massacres without a thought.
War.
All life it hates.
War.

Shells exploding,
Life declining,
Weapons firing,
War is rising.

Broken treaties.
Invasion.
Battles.
Death.
Innocence and weakness,
All lead to the uprise of
War!

Jack Price (10)
South Farnborough Junior School

A FOOTBALL FAN

I am a big football fan
I watch it all the time,
To become a football player
Is a dream of mine.

Spurs are my favourite
I'd like to play for them,
I'd like to think I will one day
But who knows when.

If I practice hard enough
And try my very best,
I'll become a football legend
Just like George Best.

Jack Davis Brewer (10)
South Farnborough Junior School

POETIC VOYAGE

J   umping on the moon,
O   rbiting the sun,
U   ranus in the sky,
R   ockets flying by.
N   eptune is a planet,
E   clipses are very dark,
Y   uri Gagarin was a Russian cosmonaut.

T   he moon travels around us,
H   aving fun, exploring the aircraft,
R   oaring through the Milky Way,
O   ver planets,
U   nder stars,
G   racefully flying slowly,
H   igh in the sky.

S   eeing stars through a telescope,
P   utting on space boots,
A   pollo XIII taking off,
C   old in the atmosphere,
E   nding. Slowly we land.

Louise Harding (11)
South Farnborough Junior School

THE ROLLER COASTER

The roller coaster creaks,
You can hear lots of shrieks,
People go very fast,
They hope the ride can last.

The air whistles,
As you go round twizzles,
Your heart goes pop,
As you reach the top.

As you shoot to the ground,
You hear a screaming sound,
As the wheels squeak,
Your tummy feels weak.

You go round a bend,
You're coming to the end,
When you leave through the gate,
You can't walk straight!

Declan Pollock (10)
South Farnborough Junior School

MY JOURNEY TO SCHOOL . . .

On my journey to school one day,
I walked past some shops.
I could smell melting chocolate,
I liked it lots.

I stopped and looked through the window,
At slabs of piled chocs.
They looked so tasty and delicious,
I could eat pots and pots.

Then I stopped thinking of wonderful dreams,
Although it might come true.
I like my chocolate very much,
And I bet you do too.

Chloé Darrah-Cliffe (11)
South Farnborough Junior School

TO FLORIDA BY SEA

T   he journey and the sun both add to the fun
H   eat is a pleasure compared to the English weather
E   ating the food will change your attitude

J   oy to the sea
O   h look, a dolphin family
U   nder the sea many creatures live happily
R   elax and have a drink
N   o this boat shall not sink
E   ye-catching experience
Y   ou know I have never been on a boat before

T   ea would be nice
O   ctopus and squid, what's the difference? Oh, ink.

F   amilies are enjoying the trip
L   aws are different
O   n the way Dad said that we
R   eally are going to Disneyland
I   n the States
D   ad, I feel sick
A   nd I have just arrived in Florida.

Adrian Earle (11)
South Farnborough Junior School

MYSTERIOUS ISLAND

There I look out to sea,
And see a reflection of me,
In a cabin so gloomy and grey,
A storm is brewing on this day.

I see an island dim and deserted,
In an instant my mind is diverted,
My goal is to reach the island alive,
It is my only chance to survive.

I wake up to the taste of sand,
On this weird and mysterious land,
Lions and tigers surround me,
But everything seems hazy.

A bump on my head, things are not what they seem,
Could this have been some kind of dream?
The air is filled with the smell of rum,
There is no mistaking the pirate's hum.

Robert Harral (11)
South Farnborough Junior School

MY JOURNEY

I'm going on a journey,
I know it will be far.
But when I come back,
I'll know where you are.
When I travel far away,
I hope
You'll think of me every day.

Kurtis Wayne-Scaife (11)
South Farnborough Junior School

ANIMALS

The tiger is a beautiful creature
If you're not careful he will come and eat you.

The penguins like to skate on ice
But the killer whale is not so nice.

The cheetah runs very fast
If you race him you will come last.

The great white is a powerful shark
He may come and get you in the dark.

Steven Schafer (9)
South Farnborough Junior School

PRINCESS TIPPYTOES

Princess Tippytoes is my cat,
She has milk chocolate stripes and is certainly not fat!
Her paws are smooth and soft,
She is always curious to jump into the loft.

She has such beautiful bright green eyes,
Sure she looks so very knowing and wise,
She is great fun and sometimes trouble,
But she's always home for a *big, big* cuddle!

Tiffany Walker (10)
South Farnborough Junior School

TRIP TO SPAIN

I'm on a plane
Off to Spain
The passengers are insane
They're jumping around
Making lots of sound

I try to sleep
Without a peep
To see if we're
There in Spain
Oh this is a pain
I want to get to Spain

The passengers are asleep at last
I said to myself better get to sleep
And forget about the past
Daytime came, the sun rose bright
And gave me a fright
But then I saw Spain
The best bit that's ever happened on this plane.

Craig Andrew Scoular
South Farnborough Junior School

THE FINAL FRONTIER

S   is for Saturn, a planet we may pass,
P   is for planets and stars everywhere,
A   is for astronaut that flies through the void,
C   is for comets we must avoid,
E   is for the expanse beyond the Earth's atmosphere
    in which the galaxies exist

Lucy North (10)
South Farnborough Junior School

MY FIRST VOYAGE

We left the harbour all broad and happy
But later on we were less so chatty.
The crashing waves against the boat
I wondered how we were still afloat.
The howling wind and the whistling rain
It put us all on a lot more strain.
Water was on the slippery decks . . .
Running through them we were risking our necks.
All we could see was sea for miles . . .
More and more of us lost our smiles.
All the food was swarming with rats . . .
I would rather eat wooden mats.
I could finally see the docks in sight
All our hopes had a little more bite.
When at last we were safe at shore
I wondered if we would sail anymore.

Morgan King (11)
South Farnborough Junior School

SEARCHING FAR AND WIDE

As I search far and wide
Above the seas
Beneath the skies.

As you swim through the sea
Swimming beneath the deep blue sea.

I've sailed for miles and miles
In search of one of your smiles.

David Jones (10)
South Farnborough Junior School

THE JOURNEY OF MIGRATION

The swallow looked up in the cold winter sky,
And thought to himself should he fly or stay and die.
So he soared from his nest into the clouds,
As all the other birds cried out loud,
'Let's fly to the south!'

He flew higher and longer till he came to the sea,
He flew higher and longer and said, 'Look at me!'
The journey was very long and cold,
We will never make it unless we are bold,
'Let's fly to the south!'

On our way we were forced by some geese to go another way,
They were bigger than we were so we did not stay,
Our journey changed and now was longer,
So we all struggled on and we had to be stronger,
'Let's fly to the south!'

After our long flight and our horrible fright,
We saw a wonder delight,
The beaches were hot and the seas were cold,
At last we have made it we were told.
We had made it to the south!

Robert Murray (10)
South Farnborough Junior School

THE HEDGEHOG POEM

Please don't run me over
I'd like to stay alive,
Please don't run me over
I would not want to die.

Please don't run me over
I'd like to stay alive,
Please don't run me over
I've got feelings inside.

Robert Harding (9)
South Farnborough Junior School

AROUND THE WORLD!

In the year of 2000
The Olympic Games,
That were set in Sydney
It was worth the fame.

I was set on a trip around the world
The prize was more than just some gold,
In a ship; very posh indeed
I was obviously ahead, I was in the lead.

The night had come
A day had passed,
A long one too
Alone at last!

The very next day, I set my sail
Even though there was a blustery gale,
When I reached my destination
I saw it was the world's largest nation.

Ten miles were left
Amid glorious sunshine,
I returned back home
The prize was mine.

Hannah Bryant (10)
South Farnborough Junior School

AYE, AYE CAPTAIN

'Aye, aye Captain'
All my crew mates shout,
As they all run about
I look over the side,
And see.
I see the turtles floating,
As the fishermen go boating.
The horses' manes are foaming,
As the dolphins are diving.
I can just see the seals dancing
And the porpoises prancing.
As I wasn't watching
We hit a huge rock.
As I'm sinking under water,
I enjoy my life flashing past.

As mysteries are uncovered from beneath the deep.

Emily Hazeldine (10)
South Farnborough Junior School

THE SHIP

One day I set sail upon the sea
With my dog Sally in a tall ship
I looked at Sally, she looked at me
We waved goodbye to our families.

Further on our journey, oceans away
Hunger came upon us, our tummies rumbling
To the restaurant we went, to eat all day
The hours passed by, our bedtime was nearing.

I awoke too quickly in the night
Because it was such a terrible fright
Waves were crashing, the ship was swaying
And all I could think of was to go home.

Aimée Davison (10)
South Farnborough Junior School

ALIENS LIVE IN MY TOILET!

I was off to clean the toilet
And that's when I saw them
Tiny little aliens in the water
Right at the bottom

They were all different shapes and sizes
One was the size of an ant!
One was a total weirdo
And I named that one Pants.

The biggest one was very big
In fact, the size of a jelly bean
He was wearing a Lego crown
And it was obvious he was king.

I got a spoon from the kitchen
And tried to get them out,
But they gathered round and pulled,
And they pulled so hard that they pulled off the poor spoon's snout.

Then they started having babies
I counted them, there were four
Then we got a new toilet
And they lived in the old one, ready to invade more.

Shaun Tobin (9)
South Farnborough Junior School

MONKEY BUSINESS

Walking through the jungle I looked around to see,
A great big, hairy monkey staring down at me.

He followed me over the rounded hill,
So I decided to give him a name - Bill.

I looked up in the brightly coloured trees,
To my surprise I saw another monkey watching me.

Suddenly I felt this weird thing growing out of my back - a tail!
Then the monkeys and I had to bail.

All at once I climbed up a tree
And I grew a habit to eat bananas,
And my family didn't recognise me.

I was a monkey!

Sophia Jarvis (10)
South Farnborough Junior School

SEA FEVER

I must down to the seas again to the choppy waves and the sky,
And all I ask is the waves spit and the seagulls screaming high,
And the winds whistle and the clouds dance and the sun's
                                        sphere scorching,
And waves slap on the ship's side and the great sails launching.

I must down to the seas again, for the wisp of the flinking surf,
Is a quick wisp and sharp wisp that never will be curbed,
And all I ask is a snug quilt with bedtime stories from the deep,
And the slushing and slashing going on outside, taking me to sleep.

Jessica Berry (11)
South Farnborough Junior School

IN A HOT AIR BALLOON

In a hot air balloon, you can see anything through the deep blue sky,
As you slowly drift through the sky,
You could see an amazing forest fire,
Stripping the woods of its trees.

In a hot air balloon, you could see a fantastic funfair,
A sensational music concert or even a thrilling air show,
With all kinds of different planes.

In a hot air balloon, you could see a safari park,
With lots of wild animals,
Zebras, lions, hippos or maybe a giraffe as tall as an old oak tree,
Or a bungee jump.

You could see all of this on a trip in a hot air balloon.

David Pitkin (11)
South Farnborough Junior School

THE DISCOVERY

We've been going for nearly a day
If we run out of food we will pay
I had men cleaning the floor
As we had no food
It made us want more
The sky was turning dark
We went on more and saw an ark
Just over the sea
I looked back and thought,
'Why, it was me.'
It looked like an island
It was different.

Steven Izzard (10)
South Farnborough Junior School

DOLLY

I have a pet dog called Dolly
We call her that 'cause she's jolly.
She's brown and black
And she's a jack
She's got little brown toes
And a lovely wet nose
Little bob tail
A big loud tail
Likes to run
Play until the end of day
We stroke her head
Then she's goes to bed.

Poppie Turner (10)
South Farnborough Junior School

THE DOLPHIN AND THE SEA

There was a dolphin
So small and sweet
And she lived under the sea
With Paul and Pete
But she loved to play
And swim every day
When she went through the sea
She was always so happy
Also she was called Amy
That's why she loved to swim
In the deep blue sea.

Josie Wyatt (10)
South Farnborough Junior School

MY VOYAGE

My voyage is along the lonely seas,
Where I can be,
Alone with me,
Along the lonely seas.

As I float by,
There is a sigh,
As I lie,
Along the lonely seas.

I can't help but wonder,
What is yonder,
Along the lonely seas.

Stacie Humm (10)
South Farnborough Junior School

FLYING ACROSS THE SKY

A   s we fly across the sky
E   verybody says it's high
R   oaring off to another country
O   ver the sea so high
P   eople are all excited
L   anding later, don't worry
A   nother hour until we land
N   othing but fun now
E   njoying the sights and sounds

Phoebe Coffey (10)
South Farnborough Junior School

THIS IS THE LIFE FOR ME

Aye, aye, me matey, come, come near,
If by any chance you want to hear
About me voyage I've had so far,
First I'll just stop for one at the bar.

I've been through crashing waves,
Also found some dark and dingy caves.
I've been on adventures and seem some horrible monsters,
Once I bumped into a three-legged eye, which *doesn't* eat lobsters.

By the way me name is Peg Leg Silver,
Me favourite meal is ham and liver.
I have a parrot on me shoulder,
I am the ship's cargo loader.

We go to lots of different places all the time,
We deal with lots of things and I get paid a dime.
All we shipmates have a gamble,
With the winnings I buy the wine of bramble.

The sea is calm, the sea is rough,
All we sailors have to be tough.
We have to be up early in the day,
So that we get all of our pay.

I love the sea creatures, the way they swim,
Especially dolphins, I just want to jump in.
You have to be careful once you leave the docks,
The sea can pull you to the dangerous rocks.

The sea with dancing horses of foam,
Guides me to where I want to roam.
Out here on the sea sometimes I feel alone,
I'm glad when I finally get to my home.

Hazel Oakes (11)
South Farnborough Junior School

THE VOYAGE

I'm on a voyage to the Isle of Wight,
I'm halfway there, still nothing in sight.
It starts to get stormy
The sea rushes towards me.
I'm on a voyage to the Isle of Wight,
The sun comes out very bright.
I'm safe on my boat,
Wrapped up in my warm coat.
I'm on a voyage to the Isle of Wight,
In the distance, a flashing light.
There are other boats floating by,
And fluffy clouds in the sky.
I'm on a voyage to the Isle of Wight,
It is nearly night.
The sun goes down,
And it's cloudy all around.
I'm on a voyage to the Isle of Wight,
The clouds have gone out of sight.
It is now morning,
And I have started yawning.
I'm on a voyage to the Isle of Wight,
The Isle of Wight is now in sight.
I see the trees,
Blowing in the breeze.
This is the end of my voyage to the Isle of Wight.

Samantha Mason (11)
South Farnborough Junior School

VOYAGE

I am a savage pirate,
Blackbeard be my name,
I have a crew of twenty,
And play a wicked game.

I am not like Robin Hood,
I keep all that I steal,
But I make sailors walk the plank,
To give the fish a meal.

I make myself look good,
With firecrackers in fake hair.
I have many an amount of boats I own,
And many an amount I share.

I fly the skull and crossbones,
And sail the Seven Seas,
The Spanish fleet spies on me,
They fall down on their knees.

Any ship's cargo is our aim,
And once we have taken that,
The ship then goes up in flames
And we sail through the floating rat!

Perhaps one day they'll catch me,
And hang me from the mast,
And until that day I will regret,
My cruel and evil past . . .

Tom McCrudden (11)
South Farnborough Junior School

BABY EMILY

Her feet are small and crinkly
Her toes stretch out.
Her legs are bandy and wiggly
Stretching when she cries.
Her body is red and warm.
It goes in and out.
Her arms wiggle about
And they are quite skinny.
They look as if they're purple.
Her hands crumple up
And they peep out of her sleeve
Like they're hiding from her feet.
Her fingers are sometimes fingering.
They look like long tentacles.
Her fingernails are tiny and delicate.
Her head is floppy, small
And has soft cheeks.
Her head is very precious
Like she has no control over it.
Her eyes are gleaming, blue and staring
Looking for some food.
Her hair is wispy, soft and silky
Like the finest velvet.
Her skin is smooth and some is wrinkly
And feels like a peach's skin.

Sophie Mason (9)
South Farnborough Junior School

ANIMAL KINGDOM

I love the animals in the animal kingdom
It's nice they have their freedom
There are wild boar
The hippos, they snore!
There's also snakes galore
Monkeys swinging from the trees
Elephants walking with ease
I love the animals in the animal kingdom
The tropical birds, they like to sing
The lion is certainly king
Grazing zebra with their stripes
Are looking out for cheetahs in fright
I love the animals in the animal kingdom
The vultures are out looking for food
They do not care, they're very rude
Especially when they're in a mood
I love the animals in the animal kingdom
It's nice they have their freedom.

Louise Stone (9)
South Farnborough Junior School

THE POND

The fountain spurts water through the air
As birds are flying everywhere.
A rainbow shines through the air
As I watch the fishes feed.

The tranquil water disturbed by ducks
Trying to avoid pigeon muck.
Noisy frogs,
Barking dogs.

Children round the pond,
That of which they are very fond.
Frogs jumping from lily pads
Making me feel very glad.

Liam Sheringham (9)
South Farnborough Junior School

FOOTBALL MAD

I'm football crazy
I'm football mad
I'm Man City crazy
I'm Man City mad

I'll support Man City till I die
Through the sun and rain
Through the tears and joy
Man City till I die

I'm football crazy
I'm football mad
I'm Man City crazy
I'm Man City mad

All the teams play in different colours
Like red, blue and green
The different teams like
Chelsea, Man Utd, Arsenal and Leeds

I'm football crazy
I'm football mad
I'm Man City crazy
I'm Man City mad

Luke Taylor (9)
South Farnborough Junior School

RABBITS POEM

Rabbits like to run
Rabbits like to eat
They are lots of fun
But not when they sleep

Their ears sometimes flop
Their fur is soft
They can run fast
And they can hop

Their fur is different colours
They sometimes have a patch
Some of them are spotty
And others can be black

Rabbits are cuddly
They snuggle up close
Some get very muddy
Then eat some rabbit toast.

Toresa Brook (10)
South Farnborough Junior School

CATS

Cats are the number one for me
They are lovely animals with long tails and whiskers too.
They are both he's and they go to the toilet outside too.
Our cats like to play
Or sometimes sit around all day.

Marina Smith (9)
South Farnborough Junior School

BUBBLES

Bubbles is a ball of fluff
She wees on the parking lot
Big white teeth that make her tough,
Small black nose, shape of a dot

Bubbles has a curly tail,
But she sure smells a lot
She has small paws and long nails
That hurt if she jumps up

She's cute and likes cuddles
She runs like mad
And makes lots of puddles
When she's being bad

Bubbles, Bubbles, I do love
But how she's naughty
Heavens above
But she is the cutest dog in the world.

Poppy Woodhams (9)
South Farnborough Junior School

THERE WAS ONCE A TEACHER

There was once a teacher from down the street,
Who wasn't very good on her feet,
One day she took a tumble
And landed in a puddle,
And got herself wet a treat.

Robert Craik (10)
South Farnborough Junior School

JORDAN

If you have a brother, you'll know just what I mean:
They're messy and annoying, and very rarely clean.

He stuffs his face and watches telly,
He likes nothing more than to fill his belly.

He'll pretend to fly in outer space
And land on the floor - flat on his face!

He's always being told off at school,
I think he's broken every rule.

Sometimes though, he makes me laugh,
Especially when he sings in the bath.

Every day he drives me mad,
But for a brother I suppose he's not that bad.

He'll take your books, destroy your room,
'Lock the door, he'll be back soon!'

I like my brother, I guess he's okay . . .

But I won't think that when he annoys me today!

Jennifer Hockley (9)
South Farnborough Junior School

TWO CRAZY CATS

I have two crazy cats
They're crazy as can be
They're always climbing curtains
And jumping over me

Eric is the oldest
He's big, black and mean
When he tries to climb the walls
It's the funniest sight I've seen

Oscar is a Hoover
He eats anything in sight
From pizza to beans on toast
You bet he'll take a bite

Jamie Wareham (9)
South Farnborough Junior School

CARA, MY PUPPY

Ten little bundles of fur
Which one shall we choose,
I think we'll take that one,
There's nothing to lose.

A small, duffed-up puppy,
The new family pet,
She gets into trouble,
But not at the vet.

Long, floppy ears
And hazelnut eyes,
She keeps wagging her tail
And stealing Dad's ties.

She's got three lovely colours,
All in a different place,
She's the most adorable puppy
With a loveable face.

If she finds my shoes,
She'll chew on my lace,
But there isn't a puppy
That could take her place.

Katie Condliffe (10)
South Farnborough Junior School

RAIN

Every day I've been looking out the window.
It hasn't stopped raining.
All the drains are blocked.
Pitter-patter, it's still not draining.
The houses are flooded, people are shocked.

Fields and meadows are waterlogged.
Farmers' crops are drowning.
What will they do with the land all bogged?
Tractors only good for rescuing from flooding.

It's raining so hard, it's splashing in my wellies.
Goodness me, now my waterproof is leaking.
My hair's all wet, my jumper's very damp
Right through to my belly.
Now back at home, warm and dry
I can still hear it pouring.

When will this rain ever stop?
We are all so fed up with this soggy feeling.
Down at the canal I saw a frog hop.
I went home and finally it had stopped raining.

Rebecca Lowe (8)
South Farnborough Junior School

FOOTBALL MAD

Football is my pride and joy
I play it all the time
Football is a lot of fun
Sometimes I fall on my bum.

I play in the park
Till it gets dark
Then I go home to have dinner
Then I go to bed.

Some people think I'm football mad
But I think they are sad
Because they don't like football
So I think they are mad.

Stuart Keppie (9)
South Farnborough Junior School

MY DOG TILLY

My dog Tilly is five months old.
We got her as a puppy and she is as good as gold.
She runs around the garden as fast as she can.
We try to keep her out of the mud, but it never goes to plan.

She is black and white in colour, with a very pretty face.
We like to take her with us to every different place.
She likes to sleep a lot, especially with my dad,
And sometimes curls up and cuddles me,
Which makes me very glad.

When Tilly wants a treat she likes a tasty chew.
She wags her little tail,
So we know she is happy too.

When I do my teeth she jumps up on my lap.
She lies on my feet and has a dreamy nap.
Sometimes I put my music on and she dances to the beat.
I have to jump around a lot in case she bites my feet.

I love her very much, and I am happy she's with us.
The guinea pig,
The fish,
And now a dog to love and fuss.

Callum Mabbley (10)
South Farnborough Junior School

WATER, WATER EVERYWHERE

It hasn't stopped raining for the past four months
People are getting wet by the flooded puddles.
The news has been talking about reservoirs overflowing,
But there are days that are horrid still to come.
Water running down the gutters really fast,
Rivers getting packed with water every day,
The seas are more dangerous for boats to sail out,
It's hard for the weatherman to tell what it will be like the next
      few days.
Fields are getting more waterlogged,
They're more like paddy fields.
It has been raining really hard
I hope that I don't have to go to school
Because when I get home I can swim in my own swimming pool.
I can't go outside because the water is like a bullet hitting my head.

Josh Pool (9)
South Farnborough Junior School

HOME'S LIKE A ZOO

I have a cat, a dog, hamster and a guinea pig too,
Plus some animals from a zoo.
There are cheetahs, monkeys, lions and deer,
They keep us busy throughout the year.
We like these animals, they are fun,
As they sunbathe in the sun.
They like to play and chase each other,
But to us they are not much bother.
My friends they think we are crazy,
At least we can say we are not lazy.

Oliver Woodhams (9)
South Farnborough Junior School

MY PETS

I have a cat, he's very happy
He's also quite a big chappy.
I have a dog, her name is Jess
She is often quite a mess.
I have two mice, they are quite nice
Their names are Dibble and Dice.
I have a bunny who lives in a cage
I can tell you he's quite an age.
I have a bat, he's quite fat
He used to live under the doormat.
I have a horse, I am her rider,
She's quite curious about what's behind her.
These are the pets I love and care for.
When I go to bed I say a prayer for.

Kim Saunders (8)
South Farnborough Junior School

MY DOG CHARLIE

My mum bought Charlie, I was only two,
When I went potty, he wanted to.
My brother put baskets over his head,
Charlie would roll over and pretend he was dead.
When his eyes looked full of glee,
We all knew he just wanted a cup of tea.
One day he won't be here,
That lovely fluffy dog,
Who is so dear.
But up in Heaven, Charlie our dog,
The one we loved is now with God.
Barking and growling, playing with friends.
Drinking his tea, the day never ends.

Georgina Winter (8)
South Farnborough Junior School

THE SKELETON PARTY

Come to the skeleton party,
where things aren't always right.
Come to the skeleton party,
where there might just be a fight.
Come to the skeleton party,
where there might just be a scare.
Come to the skeleton party,
but be very aware.
At the skeleton party,
you will be knocked off your feet.
At the skeleton party,
you don't have to dance to the beat.

Nathan Benson (8)
South Farnborough Junior School

WEATHER

Water puddles everywhere,
Jumping over here and there
Rain leaking on my head,
I wish I was sitting in my bed
Jumping in and out the trees,
Oh it's cold, I feel the breeze
Windy weather rushing ahead
On a winter's day stay in bed
Water, water I thought I told you
Not to flood the streets
And when I went out to play
I got wet feet.

Darryl Wayne-Scaife (9)
South Farnborough Junior School

MONKEYS

Monkeys, monkeys like bananas
They like munching apples and grapes too
After it you can see them have a poo.

Monkeys, monkeys like to swing
They also like to ping
They fly through the trees
As quick as the breeze.

Monkeys, monkeys like to fly through the sky
They also like to make funny sounds
And put on crowns.

Monkeys, monkeys like to groom each other
They pick out fleas
And chuck them in the trees.

Kieran Wood (8)
South Farnborough Junior School

RAIN, RAIN

Rain, rain everywhere
On the floor, on the stair
In the air, falling everywhere.
Puddles like the sea, baby's wet and soggy feet
Splashing on the street.
Rain splashing in the gutters and landing on the floor
While people are thumping on the door.
Water flowing everywhere, if it's your house, you do care.

Liam David Wyatt (8)
South Farnborough Junior School

THE CAT AND THE MAGPIE

High up in the tree,
There is a magpie's nest next to me,
And in the garden far below,
Is a pool from melted snow.
On a shed where a cat sits,
It washes itself with many licks.

The magpies sit in the trees,
But the cat has lots of fleas.
As the branch of the tree sways,
The cat has a hopeful gaze.
As the magpie goes away with thrust,
He is caught by the wind's strong gust.

As the magpie tries again to lift,
He flies so high and so swift,
And the cat staring at this king of the sky
Wishing if only he could fly,
He would fly up and eat this bird,
Now that would be so absurd.

Christopher Churchill (9)
South Farnborough Junior School

MY CAT

My cat is no ordinary cat
She thinks she is a dog
Every time she sees a cat she goes mee-woof
I don't know why she does
But the best thing about her
Is that she's nice and cuddly.

Jack Lyons (9)
South Farnborough Junior School

I HEAR A BUZZ

I hear a buzz
Of a bee
It might sting
Oh please do not hurt me
I will not bother you
I am having a walk
I do not want anything
Please go away
Please go away little bee
I do not want to hurt you or your family
Just let me stay a little longer
I will give you a house to live longer
Please go away
Please go away little bee
The buzz has gone away
Oh thank you little bee

Katherine Castle (8)
South Farnborough Junior School

MY MUM

I love my mum
She is a crazy mum
My mum is a mad mum
She is a lovely mum
She is a disco mum
She is a raving mad mum
She is a cool mum
She is a short-haired mum
She is my mum.

Katie Bartlett (10)
South Farnborough Junior School

THE UNHAPPY BEAVER

The beaver was unhappy
Because a man came
And blew up his dam

Because a man
Blew up
His house

Because a man
Made a cabin
Out of his dam

Because lots of men
Made a road
Alongside the river

Because lots of men
Built a housing estate
Alongside that road

Because lots of men
Sailed their boat
Along that river

Alistair McGhee (9)
South Farnborough Junior School

RAINY DAYS

Muddy water down the street
Soggy wet, sticky feet
Lots of people, young and old
Everyone is very cold.

The rain keeps pouring, making puddles
It plops and trickles - causing muddles
Dropping down, hear pitter-patter
We are nearly home - it doesn't matter.

I'm in my bed now, nice and warm
I've got out of that crazy storm
My clothes and boots are damp and soaking
Do I like floods? You must be joking!

Marc Gillingham (9)
South Farnborough Junior School

I HATE, I LIKE

I like chocolate,
I hate cheese,
Can I have
Some chocolate please?

I like running,
I hate to skip,
I always think
I'm going to slip.

I like football,
I don't like to swim,
I think I'll drown,
I like to win.

I like television,
I hate plays,
My favourite programme
Is 'Happy Days'.

I like hamsters,
I hate bugs,
The worst of all
Are slimy slugs.

Christopher Wadmore (9)
South Farnborough Junior School

THE RAIN IS . . .

The rain is splashing around my feet
I'm standing in a puddle that is deep.

The rain is flowing down the rivers
I'm wet, drenched and soggy and got the shivers.

The rain is pouring, pitter-patter
I'm cold, soaked and damp but it doesn't matter.

The rain is like running water or a leaking tap
I try to dodge it and so does my cat!

The rain is filling the reservoirs, oceans and seas
I'm swimming in the waves, this is the life for me.

Naomi Armstrong (8)
South Farnborough Junior School

LIVING CREATURES

In the dark woods, there are big glowing eyes
And insects flying about.

Go outside the woods and you will find a road,
There might be a fox running in the road,
Also rabbits hopping around on the hills.

If you listen carefully you might hear an owl hooting in a far tree.
The badger snuffles amongst the leaves searching for worms.
A hedgehog curls up as a car goes past.

Look up a tree and you might find a squirrel jumping from tree to tree
And crawling down again, looking for nuts to eat.

Simon Benjamin (8)
South Farnborough Junior School

DARREN'S POEM
(With help from Dad and a well-known poet)

I felt as soggy as a cloud
That floats on high o'er ponds and streams,
When all at once the thunder so loud,
A flash, a bang, bucketing in reams;
Filling the lake, beneath the trees,
Dripping and pouring in the breeze.

Blocking out the stars that shine
And twinkle of the fresh drops
They drenched in a never-ending line
Along the river that never stops:
Ten thousand droplets at a glance
Pattering the road in sprightly dance.

Nearly all mine

Darren Wynch (9)
South Farnborough Junior School

MY HAMSTER

My hamster's cute,
For she wears a blue suit,
But she doesn't like playing the flute!

She thinks she can sing a song
But it never lasts very long
For in her sleep she always dreams of wonderful things!

She may be grey
But she can still say,
'I may be cute as my owner says
But I think the poem's great!'

Charlotte Davison (8)
South Farnborough Junior School

QUIET, QUIET!

Mum kept saying
Holding her hands
She started praying . . .
'You be quiet
And tidy up your mess
You're causing me
All this stress.'
Her face went red
And she sent me to bed.
Now she has
A throbbing head.
Quiet, quiet
No more to be said
I think it's time
For me to go to bed.

Stephanie Matthews (9)
South Farnborough Junior School

WEATHER POEM

It rains in the morning and the afternoon
And when it rains at night it passes by the moon
It comes out from the clouds and on the windowpane
It runs down the drains like a horse's golden mane.
Clip-clop, clip-clop on the car roof
Pitter-patter, pitter-patter on my hood.

Francesca Brook (8)
South Farnborough Junior School

MY FUNNY BIRD

I have a little bird
She is so very sweet
I can't wait to get home
And hear her tweet, tweet

She always sits and stares
I wonder what she thinks
When you touch her tail
She nods her head and blinks

She sits on my shoulder
And pecks all the time
Even when she pecks me hard
I am still glad she's mine

Sam Davis Brewer (8)
South Farnborough Junior School

RAIN, RAIN, IT'S EVERYWHERE

Rain, rain, it's everywhere
It's down my neck, it's in my hair
It's seeping into my wellies
It's cold, it's damp, my coat is soaked
I feel as though I'm drowning.
Rain, rain, it's everywhere.

Brandon Bennett (8)
South Farnborough Junior School

THE LION

Don't disturb the lion
Otherwise it might bite
He'll dance around and say aloud
I'm having tea tonight

The lion sleeps all day
In his cosy bed
For every noise he hears
Up pops his head

He lets out a mighty roar
To let the jungle know
He's here to stay every day
And he'll never go away

Daniel Churchill (9)
South Farnborough Junior School

A MONSTER AT TEA

A monster has burger.
A monster has tea.
A monster has chips.
A monster has ice cream.
A monster has cola.
A monster has egg.

A monster . . .
Explodes!

David Wallace (8)
South Farnborough Junior School

GRACEFULLY PLAYING

Gracefully swimming,
beautifully touching,
gently swaying from side to side.

Nimble moving,
powerful body, shiny delicate skin.
Playful smile, singing voices
reaching all within.

Swimming in and out
of the deep blue sea!
Can you guess the animal?
Yes, it's me, the dolphin.

Phoebe Wynn (8)
South Farnborough Junior School

MONSTER CAME FOR BREAKFAST

Monster had cornflakes
Monster had toast
Monster had brother
Monster had Mum
Monster had Dad
Monster had me!

Aiden Essery (8)
South Farnborough Junior School

BUGS

O little slimy snail
With your little shell,
I can't help but wonder
How you fit in it so well.

O little busy bee
Buzzing around a flower,
I can't help but ponder
Where did you get your power?

O little lady bug
All red with spots,
As I watch you crawl around
I like you lots and lots.

O little butterfly
Flying round a bush,
I must be very quiet
Shssh, shssh, shssh.

O little tiny ant
As I watch you scurry,
I can't help but wonder
Why you're always in a hurry.

O little naughty boy
Sitting in a tree,
Watching all the bugs
Guess what? - It's me!

Rees Storey (8)
South Farnborough Junior School

MY MAGIC PETS

Rebecca and Jessica can do anything
From lapping and licking to swimming the Thames
Or paddling with friends
Indigo will never leave me.
She's as light as a feather
But a bit down on the weather!
Patches loves honey
But it gets all runny.
Pussy can fetch and catch
She purrs when she wants you to stroke her fur.
In the summer, when my mother goes to work
It is funner,
We turn into runners.
When we're freed
We go at a speed.
They are funny
But there is no bunny.
I'll call my next one Sunny.
Pussy is sweet and so neat.
Indigo and Patches just play, sway
And then sleep in a tray.
Jessica loves trotting and skipping with her sister Rebecca.
I love Jessica and Rebecca, their coats are like white doves
There's five, they . . . are . . .

Alive!

Amy Aggar (9)
South Farnborough Junior School

A SAD MOUSE

A dusty box stood on a shelf with a tiny mouse inside,
Tiny tears fell like raindrops from his beady eyes.
He had no friends, none at all and so he sat alone,
With his tail wrapped around himself,
Who cares? He thought, who knows?
Then one day he went exploring to find himself a mate,
He slid straight down the banister and soared right off the end!
'I'm free!' he cried, 'I'm free from my tatty, dusty cave!'
Then he heard a noise, spun around, stood and gazed
Because he saw something he'd never seen before.
A gorgeous lady mouse, a lady mouse, hurray!
He stared at her and she stared back,
He offered her juice from his big backpack.
She took it politely and they started to chat,
Then they walked together (fancy that!)
As the evening drew close by, he asked her to be his loving bride.
She agreed, so he took her to the shabby, dusty box,
Now full of pride.

Jenny Briant (9)
South Farnborough Junior School

LOOKING OUT OF THE WINDOW

Looking out of my window,
I see the moon gleaming,
I see the stars smiling back at me
From the dark, dark sky.

Wait, what was that, a fox?
Creeping over the horses' field.
An owl I hear, in the old oak tree,
Must have a nest somewhere.

I can taste the cold winter air,
Cold, dry, freezing.
The cat's eyes glow in the car's headlights
Coming along the road.

I can smell next door's bonfire,
Dying down from this afternoon.
You can see the remains of the Christmas tree,
When I look through the window.

Calum Kelly (11)
The Grey House School

MY DOG

I have a dog called Gnasher.
My dog is so cheeky.
Once he fell asleep in the middle of the road
And my mum had to go out, in her dressing gown,
To get him off the road.

When Gnasher was a puppy,
He chewed the sofa and scratched the wallpaper.
We chose Gnasher because he was the runt of the litter.
Once we bought Gnasher a collar but he chewed it.
We had to get him another one.
The other night my dog guarded me
And when I went 'Mmm . . .' in my sleep
Gnasher wagged his tail and thought I was awake.

I love Gnasher to bits!

Anneliese Appleton (7)
The Grey House School

TRAVELLING BY HORSE

Sometimes slowly, sometimes fast,
Bareback or saddled,
Rocking forwards then backwards,
Walking, trotting, cantering and galloping,
Riding through the open fields on a wild horse,
Feeling free with no worries whatsoever,
No one to bother you,
Jumping over gates and falling over trees,
Riding through puddles and bushes.

Clip-clopping all the way,
Every day, seeing people staring,
Little children saying look at the pony,
Feeling proud all the time,
Wishing you never had to go back,
Galloping through fields of flowers,
Cantering through puddles,
Trotting through bushes and trees,
Walking across roads,
Loving every second of it.

Lucy Tapp (11)
The Grey House School

THE DOLPHIN

The dolphin swishes and splashes his tail,
And he's off.
Bobbing amongst the foamy waves,
Squeaking to his heart's content.

On he goes,
As graceful as a swan,
Then he surfaces, takes a breath,
Then dives back into the turquoise ocean.

As suddenly as he started
He stops.
A boat glides overhead . . .
A fishing boat.

His shiny nose breaks the surface
Of the white, frothy waters,
But the boat and his meal
Have gone.

Lucy Wiles (10)
The Grey House School

WHEN I WENT TO THE MOON

When I floated up to the moon,
I tried to eat ice cream with my spoon.
It floated up into the air,
I really thought it wasn't fair!

For lunch we had some Cheddar cheese,
Then I got asthma and started to wheeze.
The spaceship crashed but first thing's first,
How do I get back to Earth?

I'm stuck in this deserted place,
With a broken shoe and a frayed lace.
There's some astronauts, 'Look here, please!'
They just looked back and shouted, 'Cheese!'

I saw a mini flying saucer,
Inside I saw young Geoffrey Chaucer.
Then he shot magic from his gun,
And turned me into a currant bun.

Michael Gilks (9)
The Grey House School

SPIDERS

I got a spider catcher for Christmas.
Until then I hated spiders.
Then I used to hunt for spiders around the house.

Hunting spiders,
There, everywhere.
Hunting spiders,
There, everywhere.

They're all in the corners.
All you have to do is look.
They jump out at you
But I'm ready to catch them.

Hunting spiders,
There, everywhere.
Hunting spiders,
There, everywhere.

The next day I found one
In my sea monkeys,
So I fished him out.

Hunting spiders,
There, everywhere.
Hunting spiders,
There, everywhere.

Now I've got a spider catcher
I'm really brave.
But sometimes I can't reach them,
So I ask my dad!

Emma Yeoman (8)
The Grey House School

A BUMP IN THE NIGHT

There was a bump in the night
Tap, tap, tap
I crept downstairs and I heard
A bang! Bang! Bang!

I looked around everywhere
I couldn't see anything or anyone
I turned cold
Thump, thump, thump.

I crept upstairs
Getting redder and redder
I heard a creak
I ran upstairs.

'Mum! Mum!
I heard things downstairs.'
'You must have been dreaming.'
'I wasn't! I wasn't!'
'Go back to bed.'

I crept slowly to my bed
Tick-tock, it was my clock
I huddled up in my bed
And rested my head on my bed

I couldn't sleep
I kept on wondering
When I would hear it again.
Tap! Bang! Thump!

I was so red and cold
I almost felt like crying
I decided to be brave
Then relaxed and slept.

Christopher Pitcher (9)
The Grey House School

THE CAT

The cat walks slowly
across the grass
turning its head
from side to side
looking for its prey.
The grass is damp
and the cat picks up the mud
on its soft, padded paws.
Suddenly it spots something.
It crouches low
ready to pounce.
The animal runs,
the cat jumps high.
It lands heavily on the grass
and catches the creature -
but it is not dead.
The cat's claws shine viciously
and frighten the animal.
It struggles and escapes
It runs wildly into the woods.
The cat is not pleased
so it chases after it.
But it's too late.
The animal has got away.
The cat, sulking, walks back
to the end of the garden
and waits quietly behind a bush
for its next lot of prey.

Daisy Prowse (10)
The Grey House School

ROBOT WARS

Robot Wars is a TV programme
But it feels real to me,
It's on a Friday night
It feels real to me.

There are bangs and crashes
But it feels real to me,
There are explosions and fire!
It feels real to me.

Fighting and blowing up!
But it feels real to me.
There are horrible weapons
It feels real to me.

Spikes and chainsaws
But it feels real to me.
Axes and flame throwers
It feels real to me.

Monster robots
But it feels real to me.
Fighting to win
It feels real to me.

Is it a TV programme?
I will never know.

George Barnes (9)
The Grey House School

NEWCASTLE

A ship full of coal heading straight to Norway,
like a black floating island.
The Newcastle bridge is steel, standing high,
like Sydney Harbour Bridge.

The River Tyne flows through the city,
like a blue worm on the pavement.
Sting is singing in the cold weather echoing
round the whole big city.

The Newcastle United Football Club stadium
looks at you with fifty-two thousand people in it.
The third biggest stadium in England,
the players come out of the changing rooms.

First to come is Shearer then Given, Dyer, Cordone
Cort, Solano, Bassedas, Goma
Dabizas, Speed and Barton.
It looks like we're playing against the Swampies.

Like black and white ants against the red ants
playing on a green leaf
and they are kicking a microscopic piece of paper.
The rain is starting hard, almost sleet.

The rally is also starting,
all the cars skidding everywhere in the thick brown mud.
The forest gets dark and well, kind of scary
but Newcastle is a great city!

Tom Stevens (9)
The Grey House School

THE RACE

The red lights go,
The atmosphere is tense.
No one knows when the green lights will flash
And *go!* The engine revving stops, instead they roar!

Wheelspin starts, the cars start moving.
Vroom! The drivers hit speeds of hundreds,
Overtaking and pushing around the first corner,
The crowd roar and cheer,
Then it really moves.

The cars quick as lightning
Multiply their speeds, they zoom off!
Then around and back again for the end of the first lap.
Repeated again and again.

Then they fight for the pits
The mechanics fast as lightning.
Old wheels off, new wheels on.
Flags wave as they get to the crucial stages.

They wait for the first driver to finish.
Zoom, he comes in as the chequered flag is waved.
The crowd stand up to cheer!
Repeated for every driver.

They're on the rostrum, waving
And collect beautiful trophies.
They shake the champagne bottles up
And spray it in their faces.

Guy Kelly (9)
The Grey House School

THE FINAL GAME

The final game, a big event
Crowds are roaring through the stadium.
Old Trafford is the stadium for the match
The game is between Manchester United and Arsenal.

Last game of the season, so much on the line.
The Premier League title.
Teams walk out, fans go crazy.
The referee blows the whistle to start the game.

Passes come in from both angles but there was nobody to score.
The managers shout out tactics to their players.
But then Arsenal scores, Manchester United cry in disbelief.
The half-time whistle went, Arsenal are as happy as could be.

Teams come out for the second half.
Manchester United take the ball up the field.
Then a hard tackle goes in and then the referee gives a red card.
Free kick on the edge of the box.
The ball gets kicked and it's . . . a goal!
Manchester United go crazy.

Near the end of the game and then the whistle goes.
Extra time was needed to decide the game but no goals.
The whistle goes. Still no change.
The game went into penalties.

One by one they hit them in. Arsenal's fifth penalty and he . . . misses.
Manchester United scored.
The title was Manchester United's again.
They won the game!

Timmy Wood (9)
The Grey House School

CARS

Cars, cars, we use them every day
Start them up and drive away
Anywhere we want to go.

They take us through water, mud
And slide on ice
We don't know how lucky we are
People had to walk or ride on horses.

It's amazing, we start them up
And take the handbrake off
Put it in gear and push the accelerator
And we're off down the long roads
To the motorway, dual carriageway and country lanes.

You can get cars blue, white, pink, red, orange
Any colour you want
You get different makes
BMW, Jaguar, Ford, Lotus, Porsche and Ferrari.

They travel at different speeds, slow, fast
They take different petrol
Some cars are diesel
Cars are like people and animals
We're all different.

The bad thing about cars
Is pollution and global warming
But I still like them
Very lucky because we have cars.

Peter Snowdon (10)
The Grey House School

My Dog

My dog is called Snoopy
Because when we got him he was so nosy
His nickname is Snoops
He is 14 years old.

We got him because my sister has always been afraid of dogs
My dad chose this one
Because Snoopy came running and jumped on my dad
So he chose this one.

His coat is as shiny as silver
As brown as a tree
His eyes are as blue as the sky
And as big as an elephant.

His intelligence is so great
He can open cupboards
Push chairs and do tricks
He sometimes walks on his hind legs.

He can go down on his tummy and beg,
He can bark when you want him to.
His best trick is bang
You point your finger and say 'Bang' and he pretends to be dead.

Matthew Yeoman (9)
The Grey House School

MOONLIGHT NEAR THE SEA

Stand in the open at night,
  See the stars in the moonlight.
The strong, cool, fresh breeze in your face,
  Waves make a faint sound of whoosh, whoosh in this place.

Like a streamer the wind blows back your hair,
  The smell of salt from the sea is in the air,
The sea is a refreshing, calm, relaxed place to be,
  That's why it's a nice place to be for me.

High up is the pale circle of the moon,
  From the moonlight shiny glitters come from sand dunes.
Sometimes you just stand and stare,
  Around you as you think what the day will be like, dull or fair?

Very soon you start to dread!
  That you must, yes you must instead,
Have to draw yourself away,
  From the moonlight of this very late day.

You fear a bit too soon you'll hear the cock will crow,
  And a shining, bright light will show.
So slowly you quietly creep,
  To bed to fall into very deep sleep.

Helen Peregrine (9)
The Grey House School

THE SECRET GARDEN

I only discovered a wall
When I was five
I found a little wooden door
Just the size of me!

I dreamed only to open the door
But I didn't have a key!
Oh! What a pity it was!
I couldn't get a key.

But one day I found a metal key
Oh how excited I was!
I opened the door with pleasure
Just to see a butterfly flutter away.

I'd opened the door!
Oh what joy it was
I stepped in without a peep
I was quiet for a moment.

Then suddenly a bird twice the size of me
Picked me up. I screamed
Then he put me down
I then realised it was all a dream!

Anna Fearon (9)
The Grey House School

THE ROSE IN MY GARDEN

The rose in my garden
Grows every year.
It grows about May time,
When it is warm and sunny.

The rose in my garden
Is red, like a robin's breast.
It has the most delicate petals,
As soft as a silk dress.

The rose in my garden,
Is long and green.
The thorns are as sharp
As a holly green leaf.

The rose in my garden
Has a mind of its own.
The stamen are bright, bright yellow,
Or sometimes orange, it changes every year.

The rose in my garden
Is so beautiful.
I love the rose in my garden,
Without it there would be no summer's day!

Chloé Hancock (10)
The Grey House School

TREE THROUGHOUT THE YEAR

Blossom like pink confetti
Comes out of its dark prison,
Emerald green leaves come out
Like a lady with her flowing gown.

She welcomes the blue tit into her shelter
And helps the chicks' lives to begin
When the summer sun is blazing hot
She lets them have cool, refreshing shade.

But when autumn comes to Earth,
She lets the Devil get the better of her,
He takes her gown away
And leaves her cold and bare.

Now she's a witch with spindly fingers
In a blood-curdling, haunting wood,
Making a brew of fear and sadness
For anyone who comes by.

But now it's spring and she's back again
Making joy for passers-by,
In her emerald gown she starts again
The cycle of her life.

Caroline Haines (10)
The Grey House School

THE CASTLE

Once I had a dream
That I was a princess
And I lived in a beautiful castle
In the middle of a dark wood.

Giants live in the wood
Wolves howl all night
It rains in the night
The sun shines in the morning.

My mummy and daddy
Are looking for a man to marry me
But I don't like any of them
They are all ugly.

Once a big fat giant
Came in the middle of the night with a lantern
He was very angry
And set fire to the castle.

Then I woke up
It was the morning
I went to school, we had to write a story
I wrote about my dream.

Sophie Wort (9)
The Grey House School

A TRIP TO THE MOON

It was the best day,
Waving back to the whole world.
The crew and me.
Houston counted down from ten to zero.
We shot up in one big flame.
Running to the moon,
Like a cheetah, so fast,
Out of the window
The moon grew larger,
While the Earth just seemed to disappear.
I could see the glowing stars around me,
Like fireflies in the night sky.
The door creaked open.
Sunlight streamed into my eyes.
I gasped for joy,
I was on top of the world,
Earth below my feet.
There were monstrous mountains of moon dust,
Like a hot chocolate mix.
The moon was silent, like a deserted island.
I scooped up some moon dust
And clambered back on to the ship.
We left to go back to Earth
And splashed into the sea.
It was a great leap for mankind
But a small step for me!

Clare Henshaw (11)
The Grey House School

THE GHOSTLY NIGHT

I woke up with a fright in the night,
    I was very scared.
Was there a ghost at my window?
    'That I cannot answer.'

Was it creeping like a . . . I don't know?
    A ghost that was coming, coming towards me.
But was it coming towards me?
    'That I cannot answer.'

Was it me they called?
    I hid under the covers.
Was it me they were coming to get?
    'That I cannot answer.

Was it a ghostly night?
    The trees were very, very high.
Did Mum and Dad hear me scream?
    'That I cannot answer.'

But then I woke up,
    My mum came in my bedroom and said,
'Are you alright?'
    'That I cannot answer.'

Lucy Holman (10)
The Grey House School

DISASTER, 1912

On the 10th of April, 1912
The floating palace set sail,
And nobody thought on this glorious day
That this maiden voyage could fail.

Luxurious, unsinkable, unbelievably big,
The description was fitting and true.
But in only four days, disaster took place
In the ocean so vast and so blue.

'Hard a-starboard!' bellowed the crew
As they called for the ship to turn, quick.
Then they ordered the engines to stop and reverse
But, too late, for the iceberg had struck.

Many passengers stayed asleep
As the iceberg tore into the hull,
But the captain awoke and rushed up to the bridge
And sounded alarm bells on full.

He knows that Titanic is going to sink
And he knows that the lifeboats won't do.
So women and children climb into the boats
In the hope of saving a few.

Titanic's lights flickered as she plunged head first,
And before very long she died.
Of the twenty-two hundred that started,
Only seven hundred survived.

And still to this day there are divers
Who plunge the icy depths
In the hope of raising Titanic
But until they give up, she won't rest.

Thomas Hill (10)
The Grey House School

WHY?

Air raids, bombs,
were all people heard,
in a world of
terrifying pain.

Concentration camps,
eager to win,
Hitler over Churchill,
trying to invade England.

Jewish families
split up and killed,
not a single crumb to eat,
not a single drop to drink.

Jews being told
they were going for a shower,
but instead
being poisoned by gas.

If people
were not quite dead -
they were finished off
by a bullet.

Dead bodies
being thrown into a pit
which at one end
was filled right to the brim.

Bodies slit open
for organs to eat,
a world of disaster,
sorrow and pain.

Alexandra Waite-Roberts (10)
The Grey House School

MY VOYAGE

The crashing of the waves
Woke me from my sleep
As the rocking of the boat churned my stomach.
I was unsteady on my feet.
I got dressed quickly
To get out onto deck
To see if land was near.
All I could see was ocean
And the storms that were soon going to surround me.
Earlier the crew had held me captive,
Taken from a desert island where they had found me.
That was how I was on this boat
But my attention had now turned to the waves
For now a storm was brewing.
The boat suddenly capsized.
All the crew were trapped under the deck
So I was stranded on my own in the sea.
If it hadn't been for a passing lifejacket
That had fallen from the boat
I would have drowned.
I swam with it on for days
Until land was found.

Amy Chiplin (10)
The Grey House School

RABBITS

If you look out tonight
You will see
Lots of little rabbits
Escaping quietly.

Out of a burrow
Their ears alert
Carefully, slowly
So they don't get hurt.

They pause to look
And sniff the air
Some of them dark
And some of them fair.

The leader goes first
And tells them when it's safe
Then they follow so silently
As if their feet are made of lace.

They hop along the grass
Stopping to eat
Then back to the journey
Dancing on their feet!

Tessa De Jouvencel (10)
The Grey House School

THE VISITOR

The visitor timidly crept through the trees,
In the gloomy forest of the night.
As a gentle breeze, scattered the leaves,
And a bird flew out of sight.

He scampered across to the haunted house,
And edged around the floor.
He found another visitor mouse,
Hanging to the edge of the door.

They wandered over to a crooked chair,
Then dashed under the bed.
They saw a cat with a horrible glare,
With demon eyes on his head.

His green eyes glowed and teeth stuck out,
He flicked his tail with rage.
They took one look and ran about,
And darted to the cage.

The visitors saw a small hole by a sign,
And sprinted out of sight.
They managed to escape in good time,
Into the darkness of the night.

James Funnell (11)
The Grey House School

MY DREAM

Last night I had a dream.
I was out in the street at night,
There was a full moon
And I heard wolves howling.
I was scared.
There were wolves all around me.

It was a cold, dark night.
I was miles from anywhere.
Suddenly, a bolt of lightning hit
And it poured with rain.

In the morning I woke up
And I was in my room.

Rebecca Fisher (7)
The Grey House School

BLACK BEAUTY

At first Black Beauty was so unhappy,
He missed his mum and home,
But then he found he had two friends,
So he wasn't all alone.

His friends were Ginger and Merrylegs,
They kept on helping him.
They tried to keep him happy
Although his life was dim.

Black Beauty thought his life was sad,
Until the day came when he was sold.
This time to an owner very good,
So Black Beauty lived there till he was old.

Lucy McCrae (8)
Whitewater CE Primary School

HANSEL AND GRETEL

Hansel and Gretel lived in a wood,
With a stepmother who was no good.
'This is no good,' the stepmother said,
'We'll have to get rid of the children instead.'

Hansel left a long trail of pebbles to follow,
As he walked past the forest trees,
Which looked scary and hollow.
The moonlight shone to help them back home,
As the two little children walked all alone.

The following day, Hansel dropped pieces of bread
But they couldn't find their way back
As the birds had eaten it instead!

They walked through the forest
Looking for a way out,
When Hansel pointed to Gretel and managed a shout.
'Look over there, a house made of sweets.'
'Great,' shouted Gretel, 'We've got something to eat!'

Gretel knocked at the door with a rat-a-tat-tat,
Then out came a woman with a pointed hat!
'I eat little children for breakfast, lunch and tea;
In fact you two will be the next meal for me!'

The wicked old witch fed Hansel lots to eat;
In fact she fed him everything, even old chicken's feet!
'The time has come, the oven is hot,
And you are going inside my sizzling pot!'

The oven door open, half full of wood,
Gretel pushed the old witch in because she was no good!
Hansel and Gretel were free at last
And ran down the hill terribly fast!

Up steep hill and dale, through dense woods and trees,
They spotted their father who was on both knees.
'Your stepmother's gone,' they heard him say,
So the children both shouted, 'Hip, hip hooray!'

Emily Blunden (9)
Whitewater CE Primary School

AUTUMN HAS COME

Autumn's coming,
Faint guns going,
Birds cheeping,
Deer feeding,
Rabbits gathering,
Wind singing.

Splashing puddles,
Soft mud and the smell of misty days.

Conkers smashing in bronzy brown coats,
Red deer skipping,
Cold, windy nights,
Owls screeching,
Mice chattering and frogs jumping high.

Streams flowing
And minnows darting.
Trees whispering secrets.
But still the leaves are sweeping down
Like aeroplanes showing off.

Tim Cade (9)
Whitewater CE Primary School

THE SEA OTTER

He lives in the sea,
He eats fish.
His big wet nose shines in the sun.
He lays on his back
Playing with his round smooth pebble.
Turning, twisting, tumbling.
He's an excellent swimmer
Swishing, swirling, splashing.
His brown furry coat keeps him warm
In the bitter cold.
His tiny bead-like eyes
Watching, waiting, wondering.
His little ears
Listening.
His whiskers
Twitching.

Ben Brabec (9)
Whitewater CE Primary School

THE SNAIL

He slides and glides over concrete paths
And up the steep, cold walls.
Through the puddles, over the stones
Under the leaves that fall.
Gently touch him
Hey! Where did he go?
He's hiding inside his shell.
Leave him and he'll pop out again.
I know this snail quite well.

Cory Monk (9)
Whitewater CE Primary School

WINTER

Long greying hair, a long grey beard,
White stockings with frost on them.
A frosty white shepherd's crook.
Icicles hanging from his ears and long beard.

White icy shoes.
Able to sense when the sun comes up
An hour before it does.
Begging for spring to come late.

Spring has come at last!
The old man is sometimes seen shuffling
Across the sea
To the Antarctic where it is always winter.

Tim Sharp (10)
Whitewater CE Primary School

THE SNAIL

Slippery snail slides
Leaving a silvery trail.
Quietly hiding under garden pots
In its smooth and spirally shell.
It wakes up in the next morning
And searches for something to eat.
Looking for fresh leaves to munch on,
Looking for a special treat.

Emma Davies (8)
Whitewater CE Primary School

THE ELVES AND THE SHOEMAKER

A shoemaker he lived with his old wife
In a house they were about to lose
They had no money, not much of a life
With leather for one pair of shoes

He cut out the leather upon the table
And climbed the stairs to his bed
'I'll finish those tomorrow when I am able
Oh what's to become of us?' he said.

In the morning the shoes to his surprise
Had been sewn with stitches so neat
His wife, she couldn't believe her eyes
'Sell those and there'll be money for meat!'

He put the shoes in his window and soon
He could buy leather for two more pairs
And after this had gone on until the next full moon
The old couple had no more cares

But the shoemaker's wife, she wanted to know
Who had worked through the night with such care?
And she saw in the dark, the ones who could sew
Were two elves who where almost threadbare

'I'll make them some clothes,' the old woman cried
'To thank them for all of their trouble.'
And she left them downstairs in red ribbon tied
Hat, jacket, boots, trousers, all double

The elves put on their clothes new and fine
And danced straight out of the door
The shoemaker stayed lucky to the end of his time
But the elves were seen alas no more.

Emma Carlstedt-Duke (8)
Whitewater CE Primary School

CHRISTMAS

Berries being gathered from the holly,
Even in the cold all bright and jolly,
Red wine is drunk and then there is more,
And Santa comes down while the children snore.

Plump satsumas, juicy and sweet,
Chocolate orange, tasty to eat,
Crackers are pulled and hats put on,
In the morning the carrots for Rudolph are gone.

Candlelight makes a friendly glow,
Shining out through the window across the snow,
Golden tinsel is put everywhere,
And the sound of chimes fills the air.

In every home a Christmas tree stands,
Be careful the holly doesn't prickle your hands,
The children's bedtime is really long past,
But we'll let them off as Christmas comes fast.

Fingers turn blue playing out in the snow,
Warm them up quickly in the fire's glow,
Ribbons round presents are tied in a knot,
Undo them quickly and see what we've got.

Children gaze up at the indigo sky
And try to see Santa flying by
Gallons of ink used on Christmas wishes,
People are coming, get out the best dishes.

The violet baubles hung on the tree,
Make sparkles and glitters for all to see,
The violet sweet wrappers flung on the floor,
Are tidied up swiftly for an encore.

Benjamin Dawson (11)
Whitewater CE Primary School

WINTER POEM

His hair is ivy, it blows behind him as he runs,
His eyes are big and white like snow,
His nose is round and frosty,
His mouth is big and glittery,
His tongue is as sharp as an icicle,
His breath is cold and windy,
He smells damp and wet,
His clothes look dark, with his cloak made from Christmas tree needles,
When he touches anything it turns cold and damp like frost,
His hands are made from ice so he melts in the summer,
Winter is his name.

Jenny Syckelmoore (10)
Whitewater CE Primary School

CHRISTMAS

C   hrist was born in Bethlehem, 2000 years ago,
H   erod wasn't happy, as happiness goes.
R   ushed they did, out of Bethlehem, so Jesus would keep his life
I   n the desert they fled away, Jesus, Joseph and his wife.
S   aviour born in a stable, contented (I don't think!)
T   he mother and the father, had to be strongest link.
M aybe, one day, somewhere, in 2000 years time,
A   nother child is born, to give the world a sign,
S   ignifying freedom, love, youth, happiness and truth!

Polly Collins (11)
Whitewater CE Primary School

MY CHRISTMAS POEM

Red berries on the holly bush,
Red decorations on the Christmas tree,
Red stockings hanging by the fire,
And the red school choir.

Orange wrapping paper on our presents,
Orange satsumas in our stockings,
Orange sunset outside where it snows,
And orange blankets to warm up your toes.

Yellow tinsel hanging round the door,
Yellow Christmas lights all around the house,
Yellow angels singing in the sky,
And yellow bells ringing as we lie.

Lydia Jones (10)
Whitewater CE Primary School

CHRISTMAS

C   hristmas is a time to share with your family,
H   appy are the children playing by the tree,
R   ound the tree presents lay,
I   n the oven the turkey is roasting,
S   anta is on his way,
T   oys are being played with, the ones that have just arrived,
M   erry Christmas to everyone,
A   s we see it come,
S   o Merry Christmas to all.

Harriet Carter (10)
Whitewater CE Primary School

WINTER

His hair is flyaway, silvery white,
Glittery, sparkly light as a kite,
Entwined with ivy, sprinkled with snow,
What shampoo he uses we never will know.

His eyes shining, wintry glare,
Nose glowing, reflecting his hair,
His mouth a slit, made out of coal,
His two ears are not just two holes.

His fingers are like icicles on a stick,
If you get thirsty, give them a lick,
His feet are made of powdery snow,
When you come out, he will lie low.

His gloves are creamy light blue,
His boots are sticky like superglue,
Sticking firmly to the ground,
His house where he stays will never be found.

Rose Cresswell (10)
Whitewater CE Primary School

CHRISTMAS POEM

Christmastime is really fun,
I got a Barbie and Dad got a gun!
Christmas stockings hanging in a row,
On the top of the present there is a bow.

A beautiful angel at the top of the tree,
Presents underneath for you and me.
Red tinsel on the door,
Unwrapped presents on the floor.

Santa's suit is white and red,
Children are excited in their bed.
Christmas dinner was nice,
I had chicken, potatoes and even rice.

Holly berries shining bright,
Santa comes in his sleigh at night.
Snow is falling on the ground,
The present grandma gave me cannot be found!

Sophie Claessens (9)
Whitewater CE Primary School

AUTUMN

She lights the trees on fire,
With her coat of flames,
Burning the leaves to brown.
She blows softly
Through the trees,
The leaves float down
On the breeze.
Her eyes gleam copper,
Her gentle face shines,
She smells of fruit, flowers,
Cider and wines.
Her scarlet hands brush the corn,
And make it gold.
Her headdress of russet and ochre
Is a marvel to behold.
She battles winter
Until she is driven away.
Then sleeps until summer
Has had its day.

Simon Clough (9)
Whitewater CE Primary School

WINTER

She has hair of dripping ice and snowflakes.
Everything she touches from tree to rock.
Turns to ice and snow.
She has hands like lumps of ice
Her fingers are pale, made from icicles.
She has a pink candyfloss tongue.
Her teeth are bright white.
Her nose formed from clouds.
Her eyes a cold fiery blue flame.
Her feet a pale light blue.
Her hat made from water and ice
Slowly dripping down her.

Jade Gibson (10)
Whitewater CE Primary School

CHRISTMASTIME IS HERE

Holly berries flying around the garden,
Red wine being poured into glasses,
Stockings being hung on doors,
Christmastime is here.
Mistletoe hanging from doors and ceilings,
Grassy green Christmas trees with presents underneath,
Christmastime is here.
Christmas holly dancing in the wind,
Church bells ringing loudly,
Stars gleaming brightly in the night's dark sky,
Christmas lights are shining bright,
Christmastime is here!

Amey Welch (10)
Whitewater CE Primary School

FOREST FIRE (FIREWORKS)

Forest
Fire
Racing rockets
Glare at the moon
As a line of sparks is leaping and darting.
Then *bang* - sparks pirouette down to Earth
There's hunters in the forest!
A flying snake darts over the fence
Then burrows into the ground.
A leopard leaps from one side to the other of the haunted forest.
Then a pair of monkeys swing and go wild.
No they are not monkeys
They are showers of rain.
Silence, silence
Silence, silence.

Kerry Corley (8)
Whitewater CE Primary School

SPACE BAT

Rich black,
Black as coal.
Burning red eyes bulging, staring,
Glaring over the world.
Gliding, swooping, flapping through the stormy sky.
Tail lashing, swooping down to Earth - *bang!*
It has landed on Australia.
Hairy ears, black nose, blood dripping from his white fangs.
His shiny scales sparkle in the moonlight.
Yellow killer claws.

Lily Cresswell (8)
Whitewater CE Primary School

WINTER POEM

His eyes twinkle like the stars,
His wet, gloomy nose, cold,
His hair waving behind him like a slide,
His lips shining silver,
His ears cold as ice,
He smells like thick smoke,
His tongue made of cold, cold ice,
His clothes made of green ivy,
His hat, shoes, socks and coat all
Shine bright like gold,
He's like candyfloss
Winter is his name.

Holly Dingley (10)
Whitewater CE Primary School

WINTER

Winter is cold
Winter is icy
Winter is fun

Winter is frosty
Winter is snowy
Winter is foggy

Winter is freezing
Winter is misty
Winter is cloudy

I love winter.

Charley Storrard (9)
Whitewater CE Primary School

MY WINTER POEM

Snow whirling onto the ground,
Silver trees sparkling in the wind.
Leaves crackling on the floor,
Crystal spider webs sparkling in the sun.
Snowmen standing all around,
Snowflakes twinkling as they touch the ground.
Snow sparkling on the trees,
The ground covered in thick snow.

Rebecca Mark (8)
Whitewater CE Primary School

MY WINTER POEM

Icicles dangling from snow-covered gutters,
Silent snow curling around branches,
Snow on the gardens like silver and white jewellery,
Fields containing icing sugar.
Sun melting the snow slightly
And children tramping the fields
With snow right up to their knees.
Warm fires blazing in the snow-white windows.

Hannah Barrett (8)
Whitewater CE Primary School

CHRISTMAS POEM

Red holly berries for the cold birds to eat.
Red is the colour of Santa's clothes.
Glittering red tinsel for our Christmas trees.
A big red stocking for Santa to fill.

Bright orange crackers waiting to be pulled.
Juicy orange satsumas for us to eat.
Orange wrapping paper to cover the presents.
Shiny orange baubles to hang on the tree.

Green is the colour of the fir Christmas tree.
Hanging over the door the green mistletoe leaves.
Dark green holly leaves with their prickly edges.
Sweeties wrapped in bright green paper.

Yellow haloes around angels' heads.
Golden yellow flames in the green fire.
A yellow paper crown from your cracker.
Lights flickering yellow on the Christmas tree.

Blue is the colour of your freezing hands.
Blue is the colour of the jumper I've just unwrapped.
The slippery ice on the frozen pond.
Blue foil covering my favourite sweet.

Katie Mark (9)
Whitewater CE Primary School

TIGER

A tiger pounces like a lion,
He stalks his prey and rips it apart,
He roars as loud as thunder in the middle of the jungle,
The tiger's stripes are black as night.

Andrew Bannister (7)
Worting Junior School

THE TIGER

His claws are as pointed as a witch's nose,
His fur is as orange as the burning sun,
Powerful, powerful, terrifying tiger,
His fierce roar is frightening,
He rips and gobbles his prey.

Danielle Vince (7)
Worting Junior School

THE TIGER

Roaring in the dead of night,
Colour of the burning sun,
Stripes as black as coal,
Shadowing his prey.

Nathan Loader (7)
Worting Junior School

THE TIGER

The powerful tiger,
His fierce eyes,
His fur is as orange as the sun,
His stripes are as black as the dark night.

Molly Pearce (7)
Worting Junior School

TIGER

Hear the tip of the hungry teeth hunting!
Scary tiger!
Whisper or they will eat you into minute bits.
See the sharp stripes like scars in the dark.
Watch him hunt his prey.

Joshua Smith (8)
Worting Junior School

THE TIGER

Fierce tiger with pointed teeth,
He stalks his prey,
Prowling, pouncing, leaning,
He catches the antelope,
King of the jungle.

Lucy Redgrave (8)
Worting Junior School

THE FRIGHTENING TIGER

As golden red as the sun.
Prowling silently without a sound.
Stripes as black as night.
Howling like the wind.
Eyes burning like the fire.

Jessica Elbrow (8)
Worting Junior School

THE FRIGHTENING TIGER

Striding around the jungle,
With a mighty roar.
He is the king of the jungle,
His claws as sharp as a sword.
His teeth like a killing shark,
His stripes as black as the darkness.
His fur like an orange sun,
Cruel, crocodile eyes.

Leanne Pender (7)
Worting Junior School

THE TIGER

Tiger, tiger so fierce,
Teeth as sharp as a sword,
Stripes as black as night,
He runs so fast it looks like he is flying.

Roxanne Meade (7)
Worting Junior School

THE TIGER

His claws are as sharp as an axe.
His teeth are pointy like knives.
Roar! Roar! Roar!
He pounces very fast.

Ryan O'Grady (8)
Worting Junior School

TIGER

The scariest animal around.
I shiver and shake every day.
Get ready to run, people.
Everyone, the king of the jungle is here.
Roaring and coming to get you.
See him run like the wind.

Joshua Barron (8)
Worting Junior School

SNOW

The snow falls down to the ground
But without a sound
On go the Christmas lights
And it's ever so bright
Me and my friends go out to play
Out in the snow today.

Emma Hearne (9)
Worting Junior School

THE TIGER

His stripes are as dark as the night.
He leaps as far as a kangaroo.
His teeth are as sharp as a razor.
He creeps around the jungle looking for his prey.

Katy King (7)
Worting Junior School

SUMMERTIME

The weather outside is bright and sunny,
I'm off to the beach with my mummy,
I will swim all day,
We want the sun to stay.
Now we have to go,
What a day
I'm glad it didn't snow.

Garry Brown (9)
Worting Junior School

SCHOOL

School, school, I like school.
Every day I come to school.
I like literacy and maths.
My school is very big.
I want to come to school every day
Even when it's raining.

Amy Green (8)
Worting Junior School